Narrative in the Ballades of Fryderyk Chopin

I-Chen Chen

Narrative in the Ballades of Fryderyk Chopin

Rhythm as a Reflection of Adam Mickiewicz's Poetic Ballads

VDM Verlag Dr. Müller

Impressum/Imprint (nur für Deutschland/ only for Germany)
Bibliografische Information der Deutschen Nationalbibliothek: Die Deutsche Nationalbibliothek
verzeichnet diese Publikation in der Deutschen Nationalbibliografie; detaillierte bibliografische
Daten sind im Internet über http://dnb.d-nb.de abrufbar.

Coverbild: www.purestockx.com

Verlag: VDM Verlag Dr. Müller Aktiengesellschaft & Co. KG
Dudweiler Landstr. 99, 66123 Saarbrücken, Deutschland
Telefon +49 681 9100-698, Telefax +49 681 9100-988, Email: info@vdm-verlag.de
Zugl.: New York, New York University, Diss., 2005

Herstellung in Deutschland:
Schaltungsdienst Lange o.H.G., Berlin
Books on Demand GmbH, Norderstedt
Reha GmbH, Saarbrücken
Amazon Distribution GmbH, Leipzig
ISBN: 978-3-639-16759-7

Imprint (only for USA, GB)
Bibliographic information published by the Deutsche Nationalbibliothek: The Deutsche
Nationalbibliothek lists this publication in the Deutsche Nationalbibliografie; detailed
bibliographic data are available in the Internet at http://dnb.d-nb.de.

Cover image: www.purestockx.com

Publisher:
VDM Verlag Dr. Müller Aktiengesellschaft & Co. KG
Dudweiler Landstr. 99, 66123 Saarbrücken, Germany
Phone +49 681 9100-698, Fax +49 681 9100-988, Email: info@vdm-publishing.com
New York, New York University, Diss., 2005

Printed in the U.S.A.
Printed in the U.K. by (see last page)
ISBN: 978-3-639-16759-7

ACKNOWLEDGMENTS

I would like to thank the faculty and staff of the Department of Music and Performing Arts Professions for providing me with the stimulating and nurturing learning environment in which this dissertation took shape. In particular I would like to express my gratitude to Professor Ron Sadoff, my adviser and chairperson, for his guidance and advice which helped me to continue writing through the different stages of the research process. His encouragement, and the example he sets in his own rigorous and engaged thinking and scholarship, have been an inspiration to me. The other two members of my dissertation committee have my deepest thanks. Professor John Gilbert's guidance and suggestions are always supportive and helpful, especially in the early days when I was first working out the skeleton of this study. I have been fortunate enough to work with Professor Anna Frajlich from the Columbia University. Her sincere comments are especially valuable for the research on Polish literature and Mickiewicz's life and works.

I would like to thank my piano teachers Miyoko and Albert Lotto, who have been helpful and encouraging in my piano playing as well as the research of this study. They are always my lifetime mentors and supporters. I would also like to express my thanks to Dr. Irena Grudzińska Gross, who directed me for the research of Polish folklores and poetry. I also appreciate my friends Chien-Nien Chen, Pamela Tadross, and Jessie Labov, who have helped me and provided kinship personally and scholarly.

Finally, I would like to thank my family. My beloved husband Raymond Chuang always nurtures and helps me on a daily basis, in ways trivial and substantial. His love and support gave this dissertation life. I would like to give my deepest thanks to my parents, Min-Teng and Li-Chuan Chen, and my sister, Dr. I-Lun Chen, who have blessed me with love, encouragement, and assistance of countless sorts. Their love always supports me personally and professionally, and I would like to dedicate this work to them.

PREFACE

According to Chopin's letters and other related documents, Mickiewicz, a national figure in Polish literature, was a personal friend of Chopin. Chopin had read Mickiewicz's poems since he was a teenager and they developed strong personal and artistic links after they both moved to Paris. Owing to the same background—they both were Polish immigrants in Paris—their artistic works both have a quality of melancholy with loneliness, powerlessness, and alienation (Zakrzewska, 1999). In addition, according to Schumann, Chopin composed his ballades with the strong influences of Mickiewicz's ballads (Schumann, p. 143). It is evident that both artists had a strong relationship between their personal lives and artistic creativity.

Due to the influence of Mickiewicz's poems, Chopin's ballades are rich in their narrative of story telling. Much previous research asserts that harmonic structures and tonal process comprise the ballades' narrative. However, the style of Chopin's narrative via story telling may be evoked through the characters of rhythm, which reflect the analogy of narrative strategies in Chopin's music and Mickiewicz's literary works. At the core of this idea, derived from the approaches in Expressionism, is that rhythm is an essential element in rendering music as a logical and non-discursive language which expresses feelings and emotions. This notion leads the author to dig into the roots of the narrative form of ballade, a form with the added dimension of literary relationships. This inquiry attempts to demonstrate that the usage of particular rhythms defines the narrative qualities in Chopin's ballades. Finally, the author will, from the perspective of the narrative qualities within his ballades and through the relationships to rhythmic features, provide insights to pianists' performance practices.

This study will take rhythm as the crucial element in demonstrating Chopin's narrative as analogies to Mickiewicz's ballads. Through the rhythmic analysis this study also offers an innovative view about the formal setting of Chopin's ballades distinguished from the conventional and musical point of view. The author will utilize the following procedures: the comparison of rhythms in Chopin's ballades and poetic meters in Mickiewicz's ballads; the study of analogies in hypermetric rhythms, phrasing, and the formal setting of both the musical ballade and the literary ballad; the reflection of the emotional expression and narrative in Mickiewicz's ballads with regard to rhythms.

Although we don't have any document from Chopin's writing regarding the particular ballads of Mickiewicz which influenced the writing of his four ballades, neither did

iv

Schumann record any evidence in his articles, however, scholars such as Jim Samson, Lubov Keefer, Alfred Cortot, David Witten, and Dorota Zakrzewska[1] refer the particular Mickiewicz's ballads to each of Chopin's four ballades. General speaking, Chopin's first ballade was influenced by the epic poem *Konrad Wallenrod*; the second ballade was inspired by *Świtez*[2]; *Świtezianka* was related to the third ballade, and *Trzech Budrysów* to the fourth one. Unlike the programmatic music, Chopin didn't simply imitate the scenes in Mickiewicz's ballads but reflected the form of narrative in Mickiewicz's ballads and the emotions beyond them.

The first chapter of the dissertation will start with a philosophical background of music as a narrative art form, as well as the analogy between literature and music. The ideas and theories of selected scholars will be stated, in which the nineteenth-century music and its relationship with the poetic narrative will be emphasized. The second chapter will be a description of the ballade as a musical genre along with the history from the vocal ballade to the instrumental ballade, especially for the piano. The third chapter will illustrate the lives of Chopin and Mickiewicz, and compare their lives and the artistic influences between each other. The following fourth chapter will develop a dimensional method used in rhythmic analysis derived from the concept of Grosvenor Cooper and Leonard Meyer. The referential study of rhythmic analysis which comprises the characteristics of rhythmic patterns, and their reflection on emotional and philosophical elements in Mickiewicz's ballads, will be established based on the theory of Susanne Langer and Peter Kivy. Finally, the last chapter will have an introductory analysis of both Chopin and Mickiewicz's ballades/ballads and unfold a detailed analysis of Chopin's third ballade and Mickiewicz's *Świtezianka* with regard to rhythm.

Having performed all four of Chopin ballades since high school years, the author believes that rhythm is always one of the most important elements which makes music "speak," evoking the emotional and cultural connections with the audience. In addition, as a piano instructor at New York University, the author realizes that rhythm is a crucial stimulus in guiding piano students to understand and feel the spirit of the music. Through the analysis of rhythms, students are assisted in creating performances with meaning and vitality. In

---

[1] The particular ballads of Mickiewicz are mentioned in Samson's book *Chopin: The Four Ballades*, Keefer's article in *American Slavic and East European Review* "The Influence of Adam Mickiewicz on the Ballades of Chopin", Witten's article in *The Piano Quarterly* "Ballads and Ballades", Alfred Cortot's introduction in his edition of Chopin Ballades, and Zakrzewska's article in *Polish Music Journal* "Alienation and Powerlessness: Adam Mickiewicz's Ballady and Chopin's Ballades".

[2] In Keefer's opinion, *Świtez* was probably for the third ballade, and *Świtezianka* for the second one.

addition, they learn and experience the musical and cultural styles of the time when the music was composed.

For the reasons stated above, the author chooses Chopin's ballades as vessels for the investigation of rhythmic features in the musical narrative. This study will illustrate the resemblance of narrative strategies between Chopin and Mickiewicz, as derived from the narratology of nineteenth-century music and literature and the expressionism philosophy of music. As a result, the rhythmic analysis of Chopin's ballades can be an aid in interpretation and performance practice for piano performers, and an educational strategy for describing his music for piano educators. In addition to being a starting point of rhythmic research in musical narrative study, it will bear witness to the importance of rhythm in musical performance and pedagogy.

TABLE OF CONTENTS

LIST OF EXAMPLES

LIST OF FIGURES

xi

1

CHAPTER I

NARRATIVE IN MUSIC

It appears that it is inherent for human beings to tell stories. Indeed every human culture has its stories and habits of storytelling, witnessed in its myths of the origin of the world, its legends of the tribe, or its folk tales about heroes. Narrative, in fact, is the style of storytelling in creating the methods of managing plots. Gérard Genette, in his *Narrative Discourse: An Essay in Method* (1972; trans. 1980), considers the three main issues of narrative discourses to be time, mode, and voice; the management of time, mode, and voice creates the style of narrative. For instance, the problem of "time" includes the issues of order, duration, and frequency (Hoffman, p. 277).

This study argues that music, like literature, creates its own expression of storytelling. The structural management of harmony, rhythm, melody, orchestration, and structure creates the form of musical narrative much like that of time, mode, and voice in literary narrative. In fact, a large amount of musical repertoire was associated with literature—myths, legends, folk tales, poetry, and drama.

In tracing the historical roots of the concept of musical rhetoric, Johann Mattheson's *Der vollkommene Capellmeister* provided one of the earliest and yet most fully developed examples of the various attempts to relate musical form and rhetoric; later, it became one of the most widely used manuals of composition in eighteenth-century Germany. The young Haydn used it, and Beethoven, who owned a copy, was also known to have used it on more than one occasion (Bonds, p. 90). In the first decade of the eighteenth century, authors such as Johann Mattheson (1681-1764), Johann David Heinichen (1683-1729), and Heinrich Christoph Koch (1749-1816) taught the subtle art of melodic invention and elaboration through methods associated with verbal rhetoric. The most complete guide to melodic composition based on rhetorical principles was by Heinrich Christoph Koch, who demonstrated how to construct a melody by combining small melodic ideas to form phrases, and phrases to form periods, as well how to separate phrases by "Ruhepuncte des Geistes (resting points of the spirit)" (Koch, p. 1). He stated that this organization is intended to render a melody capable of expressing feelings, like pauses in sentences or paragraphs of a speech in order to follow the process of thought more easily.

Among the musical styles that flourished in the eighteenth century, i.e. rococo, galant, and *empfindsamkeit, empfindsamkeit*[1] is the one which emphasizes on the expression of contrasting emotions. The main characteristics of the *empfindsam* style are associated with refined passion and melancholy by using the melodic sigh, harmonic surprises, chromaticism, rhythmic nervousness, or speech-like melody. Carl Philipp Emanuel Bach was one of the most influential composers in this type of style, which can be found in his keyboard sonatas and fantasias. In Example 1.1, the opening melody is shaped downward as a kind of sigh figure with Scotch snaps[2] and ends on an appoggiatura that resolves on a weak beat with an ornamented turn, followed by a rest. The complex rhythmic patterns—short dotted figures, triplets, five and thirteen notes, flourishing thirty-second notes—evoke a quality of restlessness and anxiety. From measures 6 through 10 it is the transition toward the relative major tonality, in which the harmonic rhythm speeds up and the sequential repetition adds intensity. Indeed we see there are musical dialogues between two different registers in measures 6 and 7 by dynamic contrasts, demonstrating the recitative quality throughout the entire passage.

The emotional qualities of this *empfindsamkeit* reached a climax during the movement of *Strum und Drang* (storm and stress) in the 1760s and 1770s. This movement first occurred in German literature and art in expressing gloomy, tormented, irrational feelings. Later, composers incorporated this style in their music by exploring harmonic dissonances and surprises, dynamic contrasts, suspenseful pauses, changes of texture, unexpected accents, etc. It can be observed clearly in C. P. E. Bach's keyboard music and in Haydn's symphonies.

From the beginning of the nineteenth century, the concept of music started to shift its focus to "musical meaning," as it is said, to "be capable of being understood like a work of literature or philosophy" (Dahlhaus, p.10). As we refer to the nineteenth-century music as "Romantic," Carl Dahlhaus suggests that one of the key differences from classical or modern music is that the romantic ideal in music is rooted in literature. This movement actually began with Beethoven.

---

[1] This German term and the adjective *empfindsam* are derived from the verb *empfinden*, to feel. *Empfindsam* can be translated as "sentimentality" or "sensibility."
[2] A rhythmic figure consisting of a short note on the beat followed by a longer one held until the next beat. It is often used in Scottish music as well as in other folk music.

Ex. 1.1 C. P. E. Bach, sonata H. 186 (Wq. 55/4), second movement

He says,

...Beethoven's music conceals an "idea" which must be grasped in order to do the work aesthetic justice...To unearth a constellation of a few notes from which all the structures in a movement by Beethoven supposedly derive, and to search for a subject or "poetic idea" whose depiction or expression imparts sense and coherence to a piece of instrumental music: both are consequences of the belief that before one can come to grips aesthetically with a work by Beethoven one must penetrate to a "second level" of the music. (p. 11)

If Romanticism in the nineteenth-century music is merely a term to characterize its era by referring to the music as an "emotional art," like that of *Empfindsamkeit* and the *Strum und Drang* introduced in the classical era, then the achievement of compositional techniques and aesthetic rationales would be ignored. Nineteenth-century composers still preserved the limits of form, retaining the structures of the sonata, the concerto, the opera, or the symphony, which had been well-established in the past. However, Romantics like Beethoven, Liszt, Mahler, and Wagner, offered the key traits of tone-painting, new harmonic colors, and thematic variations and transformations that generated some prerequisites for Romantic program music.

Therefore, the "second level" of the music that Dahlhaus points out above is the emotions or expressions that the music tries to convey the deeper comprehension of an "idea" or "theme" that the music addresses. As Alfred Einstein describes, "the Romantic composer was no longer, so to speak, his own poet, but sought incitement to composition in the sister art of poetry" (p. 23), poetry and literature occupied a central place in the thoughts and careers of nineteenth-century composers—Beethoven in Schiller's lied, Schumann in the novels of Jean Paul, Berlioz in the Romantic thrillers of Victor Hugo, Byron's plays, and in the dramas of Shakespeare. Liszt searched for inspiration not only from Goethe, Dante, Shakespeare, Schiller, Tasso, and Victor Hugo, but also in the paintings of Wilhelm Kaulbach. Inspiration from paintings became a fashion among impressionists in the late nineteenth and early twentieth centuries.

Modern expressionists and music narratologists, such as Susanne Langer, Peter Kivy, Anthony Newcomb, and Lawrence Kramer, develop theories to describe the concepts of musical narrative. They argue that music has vocabularies and rhythms that construct a form of narrative, and that composers, especially since the late eighteenth century and the entire romantic era, attempted to convey human emotions and philosophies through their music. Vocabularies and rhythms in music, which are usually employed in defining musical syntax and structures by musicologists, are able to create a style of describing a series of events, or what one might call a paradigmatic plot (Newcomb, 1987). This notion was a fundamental belief among the romantic composers in the nineteenth-century, as seen in Liszt's description of the expressive capacity of music:

Music…presents at once the intensity and the expression of feeling. It is the embodied and intelligible essence of feeling, capable of being apprehended by our senses. It permeates them like a dart, like a ray, like a mist, like a spirit, and fills our soul. (qtd. in Strunk, p. 849).[3]

In addition to this, the notion of an ideal of music, especially pure instrumental music, as a supreme mode of expression and the literary orientation of nineteenth-century composers coalesces in the concept of programmatic music. The romantic composers promulgated programmatic music through instrumental music associated with poetic, descriptive, and even narrative subjects, generally inspired from literature. They also reconciled music with words by enhancing the importance of the instrumental accompaniment of vocal music—the pianistic creativity in Schubert and Schumann's lieder, as well as the weighty orchestral outpourings which nearly overwhelm the voices in Wagner's operas.

The concepts of musical narrative have gradually grasped the attention of some major scholars today. The notion of an analogy between literature and music, in terms of narrative styles, has been acutely focused in the writing of Anthony Newcomb, as well as Lawrence Kramer (*Music and Poetry: The Nineteenth Century and After*, and "Musical Narratology"), Fred Everett Maus (*Music as Narrative*) Abbate Carolyn (*Unsung Voices: Opera and Musical Narrative in the Nineteenth Century*), Jean Jacques Nattiez (*Music and Discourse: Toward a Semiology of Music*), and Anthony Burgess (*This Man and Music*). In addition to these, the examinations of theories regarding musical narrative are collected in Byron Paul Almen's study ("Narrative Archetypes in Music", 1998). Based on a formalization of the concept of narrative as it applies to music, his study demonstrates the application of narrative theories to musical analysis. To sum up, the scholars listed above indicate a strong belief that music has the narrative power as literature does. Anthony Burgess, a writer and composer, states in the Foreword of his book *This Man and Music*:

What I have done here ("*This Man and Music*") is to examine in plain language those areas where music and literature undoubtedly meet—uncomplicated regions where musical rhythm elucidates prosody or symphonic structure has something to say to the reader of fiction. (p. 4)

And Mark Evan Bonds in *Wordless Rhetoric: Musical Form and the Metaphor of the Oration* writes:

---

[3] Original is from *Berlioz and His "Harold" Symphony* (1855), by Franz Liszt and Princess Caroline von Wittgenstein, adapted from the translation in *Source Readings in Music History* by Oliver Strunk.

The metaphor would remain a commonplace until well into the nineteenth century, and in certain respects, it's still with us today...the idea of music as a rhetorical art rests on the metaphor of music as a language. (p. 61-62)

They suggest that both music and literature have "an inherent structure and evolve over a temporal continuum, both have a meaning for the listener and are innate expressions of human capacities" (Aiello, pp. 54-55). A small element of music, either a motive or a type of rhythm, can be developed or transformed in varied shapes. These combinations of various shapes of small musical elements construct various musical forms, such as sonata form, dance form, rondo form, cyclic form, and etc. In Beethoven's fifth symphony, the opening theme is formed by a simple motive:

Ex. 1.2 The motive of the opening theme of Beethoven's fifth symphony

Beethoven said of it, "So pocht das Schicksal an die Pforte"—"such is the blow of Fate on the door"[4]—this strong calling of the struggle with Fate constructs the first movement and is transformed in the third and the last movement as a triumph overcoming the Fate:

Third movement

Fourth movement

Ex. 1.3 The transformations of the motive in the third and fourth movements of Beethoven's fifth.

Beethoven's fifth symphony, although in a classical sonata form, ties each movement together by a motive and follows a process of transformation: struggle against Fate and conquer it successfully. The "continuous reinterpretations" of an ordinary motivic pattern,

---

[4] This phrase in German is quoted from Anton Schindler, *Biographie von L. van Betthoven* edition 3, 1860, vol. 1, p. 158. *See* George Grove, *Beethoven and His Nine Symphonies*, p. 146.

7

which can be reinterpreted by expansion, inversion, or reorganization, help the listeners to "follow a story" by connecting the liner sequence of reinterpretations of musical elements, just as we connect distinctive events in a dramatic plot.

The analysis of music as an expression of human feeling and cultural references was first established by Susanne Langer (1953, 1957), and later by Peter Kivy (1980, 1894, 1990). Recent musical analysis has been developed to the point that it includes not only sound and form, but emotions and references toward cultures and societies. Langer and Kivy suggest that musical elements, through formal syntax, symbolize and crystallize human emotions and cultural insights. Music is therefore conceived as a collection of conventions that symbolize emotions and cultures. Through these conventional symbols, music is expressive of emotions, like happiness or sadness, referring to a certain degree to conventions based on human cultural and social backgrounds. Peter Kivy gives an example from the opening of Monteverdi's *Lamento d'Arianna* to demonstrate the narrative practice in music in his book *The Corded Shell*. The opening melody of this opera goes from B-flat down to E for the verse "Lasciatemi morire! (Let me die!)." One can well imagine a similar fall of the voice if it were declaimed in a passion:[5]

Monteverdi, *Lamento d'Arianna*

basso continuo

Ex. 1.4 The opening "Lasciatemi morire!" in Monterverdi's *Lamento d'Arianna*

Kivy believes that music "is expressive rather than expression; that we recognize emotions as features of music rather than feel them as a result of its stimulation" (*Sound Sentiment*, p. 46). He mentions the theory of Susanne Langer and the precursors of her theory— Johann Mattheson and Arthur Schopenhauer— in arguing that music is expressive of virtual feelings like grief, melancholy, joy, etc. As she states, "for what music can actually reflect…is only the morphology of feeling" (*Philosophy in a New Key*, p. 202), Langer illustrates the contribution of Schopenhauer's concept:

[5] The example is located in the chapter "Speaking and Singing." See Peter Kivy, *The Corded Shell*, p. 20.

8

His (Schopenhauer) contribution to the present issue was certainly his treatment of music as an impersonal, negotiable, real semantic, a symbolism with a content of ideas, instead of an overt sign of somebody's emotional condition. (Langer, *Philosophy in a New Key*, p. 187)

Mattheson's *Der vollkommene Capellmeister* and Schopenhauer's *Die Welt als Wille und Vorstellung* represent the eighteenth-century concept of musical expressiveness. Mattheson's book was a mentor in 1802 for Beethoven, who possessed a copy until his death (Richard Kramer, pp. 94-97). Schopenhauer's book was first published in 1818. Mattheson and Schopenhauer agreed that music is not expressive of individual emotions in the sense of my emotions, your emotions, or the composer's; however, it stands for emotion qualities or essences—a concept that influenced Langer and Kivy.

Kivy suggests that musical syntax portrays contours of emotions, as in example 1.4 where the sighing figure—falling fourth and second intervals—is expressive of sadness. By analogy to human expression, it accounts for the contour model of sadness. However, the intensity of sadness that it is expressive of is due to the fact that the figure has been associated with intense, rather than shallow or release, grief by the conventional thesis. In Gluck's *Orfeo ed Euridice* Act III, the falling seconds in the Orfeo's lament are not expressive of melancholy at all. Three musical features, rapid tempo, major key, and diatonic melody diminish the intensity of the sighing figure which is supposed to be expressive of melancholy; rather, they are responsible for the happy quality of the Orfeo's lament (*Sound Sentiment*, pp. 78-79).

Ex. 1.5 The sighing figures in Orfeo's lament in *Orfeo ed Euridice*

A musical line can resemble an aspect of human emotive expression; furthermore, music possesses expressive properties as perceived qualities of music, as Wilson Coker suggests in his book *Music and Meaning*. He argues that all the signification and meaning of sonic and rhythmic properties of music involve an "affective emotional component," and "the primary effect of a musical object as a sign is emotional" (p.1). Therefore, whether the music is programmatic or not, the function of an expressive property of a pure instrumental work is no different from the functions of any other programmatic works. Eduard Hanslick's emotive review of Brahms' First Symphony, first performed in Vienna on 17 December 1876, attests powerfully that "the expressive properties of Brahms' First Symphony must impress themselves upon the listener" (Kivy, *Music Alone*, p. 185). Hanslick criticized,

In the first movement, the listener is held by fervent emotional expression, by Faustian conflicts, and by a contrapuntal art as rich as it is severe. The Andante softens this mood with a long-drawn-out, noble song, which experiences surprising interruptions in the course of the movement. The Scherzo strikes me as inferior to the other movements. The theme is wanting in melodic and rhythmic charm, the whole in animation…The fourth movement begins most significantly with an Adagio in C minor; from darkening clouds the song of the woodland horn rises clear and sweet above the tremolo of the violins. All hearts tremble with the fiddles in anticipation. The entrance of the Allegro with its simple, beautiful theme, reminiscent of the "Ode to Joy" in the Ninth Symphony (of Beethoven), is overpowering as it rises onward and upward, right to the end. (p. 126)

Hanslick described this symphony as a kind of "expressive parade" (Kivy, *Music Alone*, p. 186), following the process of emotional transformation. As we recall Hanslick as a pure formalist from historical perception (he was a famous figure opposing the new German School led by Liszt and Wagner), he could described the very same sections in absolutely musical terms—the technical terms of musical theory and analysis. However, he chose to use expressive metaphors.

Hanslick, for example, initially described the first movement as "fervent" due to the usage of a severe contrapuntal technique. More interestingly he described the opening of the Adagio in the fourth movement as "darkening clouds." Here Hanslick didn't mean that Brahms was giving a weather report; however, he used this phrase as a metaphor for a dark emotive tone, which the author believes that it shows the anxiety conjoining with melancholy of chromatic thirds of woodwinds in the opening bars (Ex. 1.6).

Hanslick indicated that "from darkening clouds the song of the woodland horn rises clear and sweet above the tremolo of the violins" (see Ex. 1.7). Here Hanslick didn't mean to imply that this particular passage seems to be programmatic to the music, but his words are expressed as a metaphor of mood or emotion. The usage of terms, such as "darkening clouds" and "the woodland horn" illustrates the mood of natural surroundings which awakens in the nineteenth-century Romanticism with pantheistic symphonies (Kivy, *Music Alone*, p. 188).

Following the Allegro, the theme enters with joy and victory as Hanslick stated, "All hearts tremble with the fiddles in anticipation." He also noted that the Allegro entrance exudes a confident and glorious attitude, recalling the "Ode to Joy" in Beethoven's Ninth

Symphony. This description shows Hanslick's respect of Brahms' effort of tracking the tradition of symphonic writing established by Beethoven. It also implies that "Beethovenien poetic idea," which imparts depiction of humanity to the pure instrumental music, attracted the Romanticists to follow in Beethoven's footsteps. As Dahlhaus states in the introduction of *Nineteenth-Century Music*, "the hermeneutics of music—meaning the attempt to supply a unified context (in extreme cases a narrative) for elements thought to depict emotions, characters, or subjects in a piece of music—have again and again…taken as the starting point the interpretation of Beethoven" (p. 11).

Therefore, since the late eighteenth century, there has been an awareness of the expression of emotion through music, as well as some shared properties of music and language. In *The Problem of Musical Expression: A Philosophical and Psychological Study*, Erich Sorantin demonstrates musical patterns, such as melodic shapes, harmonic progressions, rhythmic patterns, etc, as rhetorical means of emotional expression. For example, a chromatic descending shape in melody or harmonic progressions is expressive of sadness. Michael Friedman's dissertation "Sorrow as a Reflection of Chopin's Onto-historical World in the Structure of His Melodies: Analysis and Performance Guide" points out that the rhythmic intensity of triplets in the themes of Chopin's Nocturnes are the sign for the expression of sorrow (p.136, 171).

Ex. 1.6 Brahms Symphony No. 1, fourth movement

Ex. 1.7 The opening of the Adagio in the fourth movement of Brahms Symphony No. 1

Deryck Cooke is a researcher of meaning in music who sees music as a way of communication parallel to that of language. Cooke's *The Language of Music* attempts to show that the conception of music as a language capable of expressing certain emotions is not a romantic deviation, but has been the common unconscious hypothesis of composers for at least the past five centuries. According to Cooke, the relationships between notes have emotional characters, like the various notes of the major, minor, and chromatic scales, and of certain melodic patterns which have been used throughout musical history. He distinguishes between two kinds of pitch tensions: tonal and interval. He shows that each twelve pitch in a chromatic scale has its basic expressive function, like a minor third as a depression, tragedy, stoic acceptance, or a sharp fourth as a modulating note to the dominant key, active aspiration (p. 90). Cooke also states that there is a tendency to associate the major system with happiness and the minor system with pain. Nevertheless, composers don't express the happiness or pain simply by using the major or minor keys, but by leading the tensions in these systems in certain ways.

Interval tensions deal with the direction of pitches. The expressive quality of rising pitch, according to Cooke, is of an "outgoing" of emotion. Depending on the tonal, rhythmic, and dynamic context, it would display as active, aggressive, striving, or aspiring. The expressive quality of descending pitch is of an "incoming" emotion: relaxing, yielding, passive, enduring, or mourning. This notion is based on the law of gravity that falling is a relaxation, and rising is an effort for man.

Anthony Newcomb's writings focus on the rhetoric of human emotion in the late eighteenth- and the nineteenth-century music. He distinguishes and establishes relationships between formal archetypes, such as sonata form and "plot archetypes," which describe certain narrative successions. His contribution to the literature on music and narrative is to recognize that an essential dimension of narrative is in the establishment of relationships between events presented in successions. He suggests that as we listen to music we "follow" the music by the recognition of subtle connections by different motives, rhythms, chords, and so on. In "Schumann and Late Eighteenth-Century Narrative Strategies" Newcomb states,

…in instrumental music one can see musical events as tracing, or implying at any given moment, a paradigmatic plot—in the sense of a conventional succession of functional events. The question then becomes: how does the composer handle this narrative; what is the nature of the interaction between paradigmatic plot and succession of events in the individual movement or piece? This issue is not purely formal-structural. It might be seen as going to the very heart of musical meaning, which lies in modes of continuation. Inasmuch as music may be (and is by many listeners) heard as a mimetic and referential metaphor, the mimesis involved is of modes of continuation, of change and potential. And modes of continuation lie at the very heart of narrativity, whether verbal or musical. (p.167)

He isolates a narrative device beloved by Jean Paul and Schlegel, which is also a main compositional strategy in Schumann's works, and engages the idea of *Witz*, as the Romantic novelists may call it—the faculty by which subtle underlying connections are discovered (or revealed) in a surface of apparent incoherence and extreme discontinuity (p. 169). In *Carnaval*, Schumann practiced this device by arranging a small motivic idea into successions that construct a larger narrative form. The structural method is to interconnect all of the fragments, seemingly separated from each other, by subconscious pitch connections, the musical equivalent of *Witz*. Therefore, a small set of pitches is used to establish melodies that are superficially different in rhythm, harmony, melodic contour, character, tempo, etc (Ex. 1.8).

Newcomb believes that music is a form of communication, reflecting in some way the experience of the composer. Music evolves patterns of mental states, as Russian formalists consider plot archetypes as the basis of novels and tales, that psychologically the composer would "challenge through the expectations of a series of musical events against the standard music forms, or against the syntax and motives of his own design to create new meanings" (Newcomb, "Between Absolute and Program Music", p. 234). Leonard Meyer indicates the referential mode as the musical meaning, like most expressionists would say:

The cardinal characteristics of a musical event are functional rather than formal…music depicts or evokes the concepts, actions, and passions of "real", extra-musical experience…The referential mode focuses attention not primary upon the evolving, changing, aspect of music, but upon the more or less constant, enduring moods and connotations delineated by tempo, timbre, dynamics, accentuation, and the other attributes of music that themselves tend to be relatively stable for considerable periods of time. (p. 43)

The four pitches as the motivic idea of *Carnaval*

No. 3 "Arluguin" in *Carnaval*

No. 4 "Valse noble"

No. 5 "Eusebius"

No. 6 "Florestan"

Ex. 1.8 The motivic ideas in *Carnaval*

His theory concludes that the musical syntax can cause emotional responses. Based on the conception of tension and release, he notes that musical stimuli, such as tempo, timbre, dynamics, accentuation, etc. arouse tendencies and therefore give rise to emotions. The emotional responses may be distinguished by the listener based on the expectations learned from stylistic norms.

Newcomb seems to make further considerations of the referential meaning in music, especially in nineteenth-century music. He argues that a psychological evolution could be recognized according to the course of "ideas"[6], which he calls "plot archetype." Plot archetypes in music may be formed by variations of musical syntax and standard musical forms, and further by the manner of constructing a musical form—from building themes and phrases by motives, cadences, and harmonic successions, to building a large multi-movement structure, for individual works.

Lawrence Kramer develops a way of describing the deeper structural contents in music through the relationship to poetry in the Romantic period. He observes that around the turn of the nineteenth century, the interrelation between music and poetry is more elusive,

---

[6] "Ideas" refers to emotional evolutions or mental states of musical events.

and the convergence of both arts has been made by the resemblance of structural rhythms from work to work. Kramer states,

> From the standpoint of cultural history, it might best be described as a conviction that music and poetry have the same preconscious sources, that they differ only in the means of representing a primary condition of imagination.

> Prior to the nineteenth century, norms for completeness were ordinarily based on some concept of rationality and modeled on forms of discourse that could be accepted as self-evidently coherent. As a rule, these discursive models of completeness produce structural rhythms that function as expressions of a coherent "statement". A lyric poem might accordingly unfold as a logical argument, an extended description, the development of an analogy, the elaboration of a distinction, or the presentation of a problem and its solution. A composition would similarly unfold as an instance of a harmonically or contrapuntally determined form—the fugue, the da capo aria, a dance form, or one of the sonata forms, among others. (*Music and Poetry*, p.16)

In *Music and Poetry*, Kramer suggests that music and poetry have been linked in several ways. He describes the speculative keenness about textures and structures of expression in both arts. Kramer notes that the structure of a work of art is constructed to externalize the actions of the mind of the artist; in other words, the structural rhythm presents the organic and re-creative values of the artist's consciousness. For example, repetition is a basic structural feature of most music and poetry. Kramer states repetition "is largely responsible for the heightened feeling of interwovenness, the tangible sense of continuity and organic relatedness, that sets musical and poetic forms apart from others" (p. 25). In poetry, the repetition of words is the emphasis of a certain feeling for dramatic purposes; for example, in Milton's *Samson Agonistes* 80-82:

> O dark, dark, dark, amid the blaze of noon,
> Irrecoverably dark, total eclipse
> Without all hope of day!

In music, repetition is often a sense of balance or proportion, a principle of stability—for instance, the similarity of the first and the last sections in sonata and other ternary forms. However, in the Romantic period, the repetition developed a new function: the "unnecessary" repetition of a phrase, a gesture, a narrative unit, or a sectional unit is a sign of the abnormal state of mind which involves distress, disturbance, or turbulence (p. 27). Kramer gives us a good example from the recapitulation of Beethoven's "Appassionata" sonata. The recapitulation is not considered as a release of tension, but it brings the tonic over the pedal point on the dominant and the Neapolitan, with an unexpected transitional measure of B-F tritones. The tonic in the recapitulation becomes an unstable form of return, and the tension is prolonged by the repetition of the rhythmic motive ♪♪♩ ❘ ♩ with its unique descent D-flat—C figure until the last moment. The recapitulation is not a resolution but a continuity of the tension. It achieves closure by reaching a point of exhaustion. Therefore, Beethoven treats repetition as a travesty on a continuous, fluent-time feeling; as other Romantics, the repetition is a "fallen" form of the same activity (p. 42).

Kramer concludes that both music and poetry are the shaped flow of time produced by the unfolding of a structural rhythm, especially where that rhythm has a cathectic basis (p. 241). The structural rhythm unfolds through the continuity of emotional alterations, while the continuity is made by the connection of different modes of discourse demonstrated by the descriptive metaphors in poetry and the harmonic, melodic, and rhythmic gestures in music. In other words, the physical design might have a philosophical purpose. The introduction to Beethoven's Third "Rasumovsky" Quartet is sorrowfully slow and lacks key-feeling. The listener is left in a complete fog at the beginning of the Quartet for many measures, an effect that is mixed by melodic and rhythmic vagueness with harmonic confusions. Beethoven didn't employ the traditional way to the tonic, but he utilized diminished 7th and chromatic voicing for an indeterminate sonority. Even the long-awaited C major cadence that introduces the main theme is prepared by an ambiguous V7/IV. The harmonic vocabulary of the introduction is entirely of Classical tonality—a few triads and a great amount of seventh chords, but with a rearranged order. The Classical procedures of tonal definition and chord-progression disappear; instead, the chromatic voice-leading connects unrelated harmonies. The notion of dominant to tonic becomes neutralized, and the focus of the progression lies on the intense stepwise harmonic relationship. Therefore, the sorrowfulness and uncertainty of the introduction is fully expressed and the bridge to the open tonic is very intense and powerful.

As a result, expressionists and music narratologists interpret music as a narrative means of expressing actions of thoughts and feelings associated with human life. "An interpretation unhesitatingly seizes on any association, substitution, analogy, construction, or leap of reference that it requires to do its work" (Kramer, *Music as Cultural Practice*, p. 15). Music, in the eyes of expressionists and narratologists, is not only an organization of sounds, but the sounds and phrases in music create a mimetic and referential metaphor to make the sounds and phrases speak meaningfully. The next chapter will show the ballade as a form that literature and the Romantic Movement were involved during its development, as well as a preferred genre for metaphors of human emotions owing to its origin from the literary ballad.

CHAPTER II

BALLADE AS A GENRE FOR PIANO MUSIC

Composers in the nineteenth century searched for possibilities to be free from the classical limitations. There are two reasons to explain this phenomenon. First, the development of Romanticism in the field of literature nurtured the minds of composers, many of whom were encouraged to draw inspiration from novels, dramas, and poetry. Beethoven, Schubert, Mendelssohn, Chopin, Liszt, Schumann, Brahms, and Wagner were great examples of that. Some of their works were written in the classical structure, but they weren't confined by its limitations. For example, Beethoven was the first one who successfully and dramatically altered the design of sonata form in his late piano sonatas and symphonies. In addition of breaking the barrier of conventional forms, they also invented new genres, which linked with the inspiration of literature, for instance, ballades and symphonic poems. Furthermore, these nineteenth century composers wrote character works like nocturnes, intermezzos, romance, or other shorter pieces that illustrate a single and specific emotion. In short, their works exemplify that music in the mind of the Romantic composers is served as both personal expression and reaction to the society, cultivated by the concept of Romanticism in literature.

Second, the revolution of orchestral textures and the development of solo instrumental music in the nineteenth century were led by remarkable mechanical improvements in musical instruments. The innovative design of instruments widened their range and made their tones brighter and more expressive; thus, composers in the Romantic period gave more attention to the complex orchestration and the virtuoso technique than those in the Baroque and Classical periods. Another aspect of the nineteenth-century music making was the modification of the piano to the extent that it became the most admired instrument in private homes and concert halls. For a century and a half, the piano occupied a privileged position as an essential instrument for both professionals and amateurs. Therefore, not only did the amount of the solo piano repertory increase tremendously but also vast numbers of piano arrangements of orchestral works and operas were published. Through this medium, music lovers were able to gain contact with large amounts of symphonic works and operas.

During the rise of Romanticism in the nineteenth century, the musical life in Europe underwent a significant change. Since the intense revolution in the design of musical instruments, the instrumental music became popular in public concerts. In the seventeenth century, the dominant type of public concerts had been the opera; in the eighteenth century, although the opera was still the primary public entertainment, the symphony and the concerto began to play an important part in concert repertory as well. During the nineteenth century, especially in Germany, public symphony concerts came to rival the opera house. In addition, public concerts in this era contained tremendous amounts of various types of repertoire; usually the standard of the program included an overture, movements from symphonies, and a solo concerto, with virtuoso showpieces and operatic arias sandwiched in between. For instance, the program of Beethoven's December 1808 concert accommodated his two symphonies, the Choral Fantasy, a dramatic scene, three piano improvisations by himself, and two movements from his Mass in C, not to mention a piano concerto (Hindley, p. 251). Of the various types of repertoire in the public concerts, it is said that the instrumental music was considered the main vehicle of personal emotion and of the expression of universal longings by the Romantic aesthetic.

Among the various instruments, the piano became the most popular one in family settings and in concerts, and was known as "the real instrument of the romantic era" (Einstein, p. 198). Pauline Turrill believes that the neutral timbre of the piano is more flexible in its expressive powers. She says,

Interestingly, the timbre of the piano tone is somewhat neutral as compared to other instruments. For example, the tone of the violin has been described as "soulful and sensitive", the oboe as "pungent and nasal", and the flute as "pure" (Willi Apel, "Violin" and "Tone Color" Harvard Dictionary of Music, 2nd edition. Cambridge, Mass.: The Belknap Press of Harvard Univ. Press, 1969, pp. 908; 856). The piano does not elicit such characteristic descriptive terms. The tone of the piano with its lack of a single specific timbre doesn't limit or direct the listener in his response to the music. Comparable to black and white photography, which is considered a more imaginative and subtle form of expression than color photography, it leaves his imagination relatively free. Being less restricted by a highly characteristic quality, the piano tone is, therefore, more versatile in expressive powers. (pp. 2-3)

Due to great improvements in piano making, the sound of the piano became more powerful and was able to create large contrasts in dynamics and expression. During the last two decades of the eighteenth century, English pianos had accomplished the perfect construction for a singing tone and for the *cantabile* and *legato* style of playing. In 1821, Sebastien Erard's invention of the "double escapement" action allowed composers and performers to achieve highly virtuoso compositions. Owing to the construction of stronger soundboard, strings, and hammers, piano works required a larger sound and thicker texture by composers such as Liszt, Brahms, and later Rachmaninoff. The modern technique for performance to large audiences was developed by powerful players like von Bülow and Anton Rubinstein (Ehrlich, p. 23).

Furthermore, by 1840s the piano had reached the dimensions and capabilities that rendered it a fully mature solo concert instrument. Early composers for the piano, like Haydn, Mozart, Beethoven, Weber, and Schubert, explored its resources of innovative pedals and escapement action; they began to write pianistic pieces like solo sonatas variations, and even chamber works with leading piano part. However, the musical expression of these works was still classical—their forms were usually sonatas, rondos, and variations. Shorter, character pieces like bagatelles, moments musicaux, and impromptus were exceptional (Turrill, pp.5-6). Since, by the early 1800s, the piano was much more advanced in sound and action, and piano virtuosos appeared in the music industry, such as Franz Hünten (1793-1878), Johann Peter Pixis (1788-1874), Henri Herz (1803-1888) and the young Franz Liszt (1811-1886). Showy compositions like etudes and variations on the themes of operatic arias were published. Later, composers like Schumann, Chopin, Mendelssohn, Liszt, and Brahms created more serious types of piano music. They didn't reject the classical forms of the piano music; sonatas, rondos, and variations were still written. However, they looked toward penetrating the currents of the Romanticism and began to create new styles of music. Thus, the piano music opened an entirely new world by the cultivation of short and compressed genres of character pieces—intermezzos, capriccios, scherzos, fantasies, nocturnes, song without words, preludes, etudes, novelettes, romances, etc.—which became the vehicles for individual self-expression.

While the Romantic composers chose individual character pieces for personal expression, they also created another new style for instrumental works—program music. Unlike most character pieces as instruments of self-expression, program music was usually associated with stories from poems, legends, folklores, or plays. Compositions associated with poems include Mendelssohn's *Meeresstille und glückliche Fabrt* and Liszt's *Harmonies poétiques et religieuses* and *Sonetto 47 del Petrarca* from the *Années de pélerinage*; those modeled on personal programs include Berlioz's *Symphonie Fantastique* and Schumann's *Carnaval*. Parakilas suggests that the common characteristic of program music is to portray a series of episodes in a particular story. Composers typically present each of these episodes by describing something—a mood or an external phenomenon—in sound (p. 20).

However, unlike his contemporaries, the Polish composer Fryderyk Chopin chose the "ballade" as a model for piano music. In contrast to the episodic models chosen by his contemporaries, the poetic ballad presents "actions in a single situation" (Gould, p. 6). It pays little attention to settings, chronological and surrounding details, psychological motivation, and description of characters; instead, the actions of the story are unfolded through the characters and the narrator's words. Therefore, the musical ballade, an unlikely episodic model for "stories in sound", is far from the program music. Chopin seemed to choose the ballad form to illustrate a story with music functioning like words. This is probably the reason that throughout history Chopin's music has always been considered poetic rather than dramatic.

Since it is not easy to demonstrate the ballad-story in music without words, the composers before Chopin didn't choose this form for instrumental music. However, the ballad form, due to the circumstances surrounding his career, was very attractive to Chopin. Having begun his international career at the age of twenty, Chopin experienced a difficult time drawing the international audience to a Polish musician. At the time, his homeland was occupied by three empires and he was always concerned about the fate of his country and the safety of his family and friends in Poland. Later, this anxiety became a desire for promoting Polish culture. In order to introduce the national style of Polish music, Chopin wrote polonaise and mazurkas and refined them as high-artistic works. Even in the scherzo Op. 20 Chopin incorporated the tune of the Polish Christmas song "Lulajże Jezuniu" in the middle section (Parakilas, p. 23)[1], although this type of genre is not directly related to Poland.

In the nineteenth-century Europe, the ballad was considered a nationalistic genre. According to the history of the ballad, the folks of local or national spirits were preserved in ballads, and this claim supported Chopin's experimentation with this genre of music. Fortunately, Chopin was usually surrounded by leading Polish poets and folklorists in the golden age of Polish literature, and in Paris he joined the Polish literary society, where he was nurtured in the presence of the Polish talents. Among those literary influences, Mickiewicz's poetry was the most important to Chopin. Since the source of his ballads was the local mythology, which was a typical Romantic, northern mythology, Mickiewicz initiated the Polish Romanticism. Chopin was inspired by the nature of patriotism in Mickiewicz's ballads, and therefore chose this genre to demonstrate the virtue of Polish nationalism. Although he was encouraged to create operas with Polish texts[2], Chopin was aware of his

---

[1] The tune can be found in *Chopin: An Index of His Works in Chronological Order* by Maurice J. E. Brown, 2nd ed., rev. Macmillan, 1972, p. 72.
[2] Letter from Chopin's friend, poet Stefan Witwicki, on July 6, 1831. See *Selected Correspondence of Fryderyk Chopin*, trans. and ed. by Arthur Hedley, p. 85. Also in the letter of Joseph Elsner on September 14, 1834. See *Frederick Chopin: His Life and Letters* by Moritz Karasowski, p. 267.

talent for piano music. Eventually he only wrote a few Polish songs, but his invention of the "ballade[3] in no language" for the piano was a clear evidence of his interest in Polish literature.

Chopin composed four ballades, and all of them achieve a cohesive and distinctive quality of melodic beauty, harmonic richness, and texture-complexity. Huneker remarks on W. H. Hadow's quote that Chopin is no "builder of the lofty rhyme, but the poet of the single line, the maker of the phrase exquisite". Chopin's melodic beauty and harmonic richness are beyond any other composers' such that his "felicitous perfection of style is one of the abiding treasures of the art" (Huneker, p. 155). His craftsmanship excelled in improvisation with a tightly organized form, Italian operatic melodies, and the technique of contrapuntal writing. As Charles Rosen praised "the greatest master of counterpoint since Mozart", Chopin's voice leading and part writing were amazing in that, as Rosen believes, they would appear "paradoxical only if we equate counterpoint with strict fugue" (Rosen, p. 285). His achievement of counterpoint came from a study of Bach that engaged him for his lifetime and that he always recommended to his pupils. In the following example, we can find a contrapuntal procedure in the fugues of Bach:

Ex. 2.1 The opening phrase of Chopin's third ballade

The opening theme of Chopin's third ballade is divided into two-bar groups: the first one starts in the upper voice and then moves to the tenor register in the third measure with the bass E-flat on the top of the high register. Later, the shift from measures 6 and 7 shows that the E-flat in the upper voice has sounded as a bass line in measure 6 and becomes a melodic note in measure 7. Chopin learned this technique that is frequently used in Bach's fugues, where the initial note of the subject is tied to the last note of the previous episode.

---

[3] Chopin used the French word "ballade" in order to keep the tradition of the Medieval French ballade (a type of French secular songs). Later the composers like Liszt and Brahms followed Chopin's footstep and used the same term for instrumental ballades to distinguish the literary ballads and the ballad lieder.

Additionally, Chopin's ballades present "definite unity of form and expression" (Huneker, p. 155), which can be examined through rhythm, thematic relationships, and form.[4] In terms of rhythm, all four ballades are in sextuple meter, and the trochaic and iambic rhythmic gestures display a natural narrative flow. These rhythmic gestures are often seen in Mickiewicz's ballads, which show the intimate relationship between these two artists not only in a personal and social level but also in an artistic one. In addition, the organization of rhythmic and melodic contours constructs a narrative form that follows the variations in intensity. The thematic transformation with the melodic and rhythmic variations displays a continuous development instead of a sectional one. In other words, although Chopin's ballades are commonly considered to be of a sonata-based ternary form, they avoid the clear-cut dramatic contrasts of classical sonata style and the conventional balance of ternary form. The flow of development in thematic transformations ties all formal sections up as a whole, which is derived from the narrative form in the poetic ballads—so called "actions in a single situation", which was introduced in the previous paragraph (p. 28). Therefore, the form of Chopin's ballades is structured neither by harmonic events nor by thematic contrasts as the normal sonata form is; the three-sectional structure is unbalanced and weighted for dramatic purposes in the central section. It follows variations of texture, sonority, and periodic phrasing, which is inspired by the stanzaic form of literary ballads and medieval ballades—narrative verses in stanzas with a refrain. The narration in Chopin's ballades—formal periods and the refrain—desists from the traditional musical forms which had been established for centuries and adheres to a form of continuous and repetitive melodic and harmonic flows.

Therefore, although Chopin is considered as a Classicist owing to his usage of periodic phrase structure, however, as suggested above, he is also a pioneer who linked up the literary forms with instrumental music. The ballade, which is a genre first used by him for instrumental music, has had a long history dealing with literature and vocal music. The origin of ballade form with the literary connection might tell us how Chopin explored the idea of borrowing the ballade form for his piano works.

The Origin of Ballade

The late middle ages in Western Europe witnessed the growth of secularism in society. The declining spiritual prestige of the Church nurtured an environment for a rising of self-confidence and assertiveness in the merchant classes and the sophisticated courtly life.

---

[4] It will be described in detail in Chapter V.

Although there was still a religious connection to the twelfth century, by the second half of the thirteenth century the profound devoutness had been gradually weakened. This social attitude cultivated a progressive tide in the flavor of secular music, encouraging the birth of new forms.

The secular spirit of the middle ages came from the songs with vernacular texts. "Chanson de geste" was one of the earliest forms in which the topic was frequently the story of national heroes, sung in simple melodic formulas. Those who sang the "chanson de geste" and other secular songs were the so-called "jongleurs" or minstrels. Minstrels were wanderers who made their living by singing, playing, performing tricks, and exhibiting trained animals in small groups. They were neither poets nor composers; they performed music from other composers' works or popular repertory. The minstrels encouraged the creativity of "troubadours" and "trouvéres".

Troubadours were the poet-composers, from the southern France, who spoke Provençal. Trouvéres appeared later from the northern France and spoke the langue d'oil, the medival French dialect that became modern French. Many of them not only composed their own songs but sang them as well; if they couldn't perform their compositions, they would trust the performance of the minstrels. Their compositions typically were written in three forms: ballade, virelai, and rondeau. All of them utilized both the vernacular and Latin texts, and their themes varied widely from the worship to the heroes, to the praise of the joys of life, spring, love and drinking. The dominant poetic and musical culture of minstrels and troubadours soon spread to the rest of Europe. In German-speaking regions, the troubadours served as the model for the German knightly poet-musicians, the Minnesinger, and later the Meistersinger, the staunch tradesmen and artisans of German cities.

As mentioned previously, the ballade was one of the most popular forms of secular songs in the late middle ages. The structure of musical ballades was established by the influence of literary ballads. "Ballad" is one of the most popular poetic forms in European literature; it has a simple stanzaic form and rhyme scheme. Derived from the narrative folklores orally preserved and conveyed by rural, uneducated people, the tradition of ballad has a local or nationalistic character. Since the ballad, unlike other literary genres, is an oral phenomenon, the style of the language is vocal and musical; therefore, it is often set into music. The poetic and musical structures of the ballads were varied; there were simple ballads and ballads in the dramatic style. Literary ballads required two or more characters, and some of them were mimed for dancing and sung by a chorus of dancers. By the nineteenth century it became a form of strophic songs, popular especially in England and Germany.

By the fourteenth century, the French developed their own type of "ballade", comprised of three eight-line stanzas with an "ababbabC" rhyme scheme and a four-line *envoi* rhyming "babC". As the capital letters indicate, the last line of the first stanza is the refrain and it repeats in the last line of the next two stanzas and of the *envoi*. There are some exceptional ballades included ten- or twelve-line stanzas and five- or six-line *envois*. In spite of its structural arrangement, the ballade is one of the most exacting of verse forms.

Vocal Ballade

The ballade was a popularly adopted musical form in the fourteenth- and fifteenth-century France. The "ballade", derived from Provençal *ballada*, from *balar*, to dance, was one of the earliest song-forms to accompany dance. The basic structural unit of the ballades was the "strophe", a unit of one or more lines linked by a common rhythmic pattern and a complex rhyming scheme. Most of the ballades repeated the music of the first strophe in succeeding ones; within the strophe the melodic procedure might be developed from line to line or might be made up of repeated or ornamented sections.

Guillaume de Machaut, the leading composer in the fourteenth century, was not only a famous musician but also a successful poet. He composed music for forty-two of his ballade texts, including the two in the *Reméde de Fortune*. The development of the ballade style was one of his major achievements. In terms of poetic form, most of de Machaut's ballades offer stanzas of seven or eight lines with rhyme schemes such as ababbaC or ababccdD. There is a tendency to use longer lines of eight or ten syllables and to make all the lines of equal length; this became a standard rule for later ballade composers (Hoppin, p. 425). In music, the treble voice carrying the text dominates the polyphonic three-part texture, while the two lower voices are played by instruments. The form of de Machaut's ballades consists of three stanzas, each sharing the same music and each ending with a refrain. In a stanza the first two lines have the same music with different endings; the remaining lines and the refrain have different melodies. The framework of a stanza in his ballades can be considered as "aabC", in which C is the refrain; this formula resembles the bar form of Minnesinger. The standard "aabC" scheme is used in 37 of de Machaut's 42 ballades, and the other five have the "aabb" pattern, in which the second part of music is repeated with open and closed endings (Hoppin, p. 425).

Both the formal principles and topics of ballades had their origins in the vernacular poetry of the toubadours and trouvéres. Furthermore, de Machaut's ballades contributed to the fashion of secular polyphonic chansons in the Medieval ages and became the pioneer of this genre. By the late fourteenth century, although there were no structural advances, the texts of the ballades had been enriched with varied styles. The praise of patrons and the celebration of historical events were often used. However, the ballade throughout its history is considered the preferred form for the serious love song. By the fifteenth century, ballades became popular in Italy and England.

During the fifteenth century, urban culture became a significant force in the arts. Although at that time the musicians were employed by the aristocrats, it has been noted that they were usually trained in the schools of cathedrals or collegiate churches. Such institutes were located in the centers of large cities, and were easily influenced by local cultures. Therefore, the treatment of the topics reflected the surroundings of the city dwellers in a realistic manner by appropriately using their expression of popular diction.

During the reign of the Valois dukes of Burgundy, the musical establishment was considered to be representative of a great deal of musical activities and services by fifteenth-century nobles and court-composers. The composers and singers were brought together for training in the schools of cathedrals and collegiate churches and would be offered positions and engagements to earn rich rewards for their skills. The so-called Burgundian composers had many opportunities to compose and perform their works in churches and courts. Due to the tradition of rivaling each other in size and quality, the Burgundian composers produced a large number of compositions, both sacred and secular. According to the deeply-rooted tradition of ballade writing, the formal structures of their ballades were regulated just as those of their ancestors' were; but the vocal part was much more elaborate than earlier works. An instrumental introduction was frequently used before the entry of the singers, as in the ballades of Gilles Binchois and Guillanume Dufay. The Burgundian ballades were popular throughout Italy, and gradually were imitated in England by Walter Frye and Johannes Bedyngham to name a few. Later imitations in Germany and Dutch were often found in the Florentine songbooks. The style of the ballade was developed in different geographic areas.

By the end of the eighteenth century, German poets began to translate English and other folk ballads and to create original works by imitating folk ballads. The composers also used the texts as musical settings—solo songs with piano accompaniment. In the following decades, the ballad continued to attract the German literature and music, a phenomenon that made Germans aware that the interest in this particular genre was spreading throughout

Europe. For instance, the Polish poet Adam Mickiewicz published his ballads in 1822, which were inspired by German and English poetry as well as Russian folklores. They were later translated into German and set to music by major ballad composers, such as Carl Loewe (see Ex. 2.2-5).

Therefore, this romantic trait in music began to appear in the German lieder by the invention of the song-form "ballad". Johann André (1741-1799) was one of the composers who made vocal settings of German ballads, and later Johann Rudolf Zumsteeg (1760-1802) excelled this new type of song by imitating the literary English ballads. The literary ballads were long poems, alternating narrative and dialogue in a tale with romantic and supernatural aspects. Carl Loewe (1796-1869) in turn developed a suitable musical setting for this type of song. The contrasts of emotion and movement in the poems were captured by a greater variety of themes and textures in music. Often a repeating stanza was established but then gradually yielded to contrasting music (Parakilas, p. 41). James Parakilas in his book *Ballads without Words* provides a perfect example of Loewe's setting of Mickiewicz ballad *Świtezianka (Das Switesmädchen)*, written in 1835, the same year that Chopin published his first Ballade. This example (Ex. 2.2-5) shows how composers of the ballad lieder modified stanza structures into dramatic musical settings. Parakilas believes that the ballad lied is closer in construction to the themes of Chopin's ballades.

The first melodic stanza presents the first stanza of text, while a different melodic stanza presents the second one of text, although the rhythm is identical to the first (Ex. 2.2). For the next two stanzas of text, Loewe used the first melodic stanza, but varied the ending each time and introduced variations of the piano accompaniment (Ex. 2.3). The following two stanzas of text were sung by the convergence of the motivic material and the keys of the first two musical stanzas (Ex. 2.4). Later, the song suddenly changes in meter, tempo, key, and melodic material (Ex. 2.5). In conclusion, the opening melodic stanzas, with repetitions and alternations, demonstrate the form of the stanzaic repetitions of Nordic folk ballads. Furthermore, Loewe created some musical adaptations of different words and tones of consecutive stanzas of text for dramatic purposes.

Comparison of the ballad to the classical strophic lied of the eighteenth century shows that the ballad is expanded in length, form, and the range of its emotional content. The piano part rose in position from an accompanist to an

28

Ex. 2.2 Loewe "Switezianka" Op. 51 No. 6, mm. 1-21

30

Ex. 2.3 Loewe, mm. 25-46

31

Ex. 2.4 mm. 50-66

Ex. 2.5 mm. 126-30 (above) and mm. 197-201 (below)

equal partner with the voice in supporting and deepening the meaning of the texts. The
demands of the ballad enriched the contents of the lied, and, by the early nineteenth century,
the lied had become a powerful vehicle of expression for composers.

Ballade for Piano

      The creation of Chopin's ballades motivated the invention of new genres for piano
music in the nineteenth century and beyond. Most of his works were new or almost new in
genre to piano music, such as ballade, nocturne, barcarolle, and berceuse; within theses
genres, Chopin created a type of single-movement piano piece with poetic, dramatic, and
complex qualities that is considered to be beyond the simple character piece. On the other
hand, Chopin's contemporaries, like Ignaz Moscheles, Clara Wieck Schumann, and Franz
Liszt, also wrote piano ballades all related to the Chopin type. Clara Wieck's Ballade Op. 6
No. 2 was published in the same year as Chopin's first; however, her ballade was much more
inspired by Chopin's nocturnes than his ballades. Moscheles' ballade, according to a review
by Robert Schumann, had a closer stylistic relationship to Beethoven and Schubert than to
Chopin.[5] The form of his ballade is modeled in a Beethovenian-Schubertian classical sonata
form, and its occasional march-like duple rhythm is different from Chopin's barcarolle-like
sextuple rhythm. Yet, the changes and contracts in narrative—the occasional wild
modulations and the connected themes—keep the Romantic trend, which has been evoked
earlier in Chopin's ballades.

      Liszt wrote two ballades when Chopin's ballades were all published. Liszt's melodies
incorporate more complex textures and ranges, and his themes and contra-themes are
rhythmically distinguished and interact with each other, which seems to imply two different
forces in a story instead of two voices or characters. Furthermore, unlike the sextuple meters
in Chopin's ballades, Liszt's narrative methods rely on the flexibility of meters—the themes
in different meters represent the different forces or ideas in a story (Ex. 2.6, 2.7). The
narrative progress associated with the rhythmic accommodation of themes and sections can
be found in other programmatic works of Liszt, Wagner's operas, ballet music, or in film
music. In other words, the rhythmic accommodation of themes allows each new episode to
have its own musical distinction, just as in the role of alternative words and narrative styles in

---

[5] In 1842, an album of miscellaneous compositions in honor of Mozart was published, and Moscheles' ballade
Op. 100 was included. Robert Schumann gave it a review: Chopin no doubt was the first to transfer the world
"ballade" into music. Only the word, however, seems new to us; the thing can already be found in Beethoven
and Schubert. Translation is quoted from Parakilas, p. 91, original text quoted from *Robert Schumanns
gesammelte Schriften* vol. 2, p. 343. (Das Wort "Ballade" trug wohl zuerst Chopin in die Musik über. Übrigens
scheint uns nur das Wort neu, die Sache kann man schon in Beethoven und Schubert finden.)

the different plots of a story. In contrast, the narrative practice of Chopin's ballades presents the consistent ingredients of narration depending on a metric stability. The alternative rhythmic gestures and the complex voicing are adapted for dramatic purposes.

Ex. 2.6 Liszt Ballade No. 1

Ex. 2.7 Liszt Ballade No. 2

34

According to Pauline Turrill, there are three types of piano ballades based on their characteristics: : lyrico-dramatic, which is romance-like in character; folk-like, whose designation is self explanatory; and the heroic, whose character suggests the epic (Turrill, p. 12). For instance, Chopin's first and Liszt's second embrace heroic characters, and Chopin's second and third have lyrico-dramatic qualities. Many of the mid-nineteenth-century piano ballades are comparatively short and lyrical written in simple musical forms. Although they may set a tone suitable for a ballad story, they do not present narrative progressions and complex voices that appear in the course of a ballad. The common character is simple in texture and form, and lyrical in melodies; the unadorned accompaniments are usually utilized. This tradition, not resembling Chopin's ballades, began with the ballade of Clara Wieck and was well-accomplished by the hands of Brahms.

The ballade of Clara Wieck, unlike Chopin's ballades, captures the style of Chopin's nocturnes instead. This ballade exemplifies a song-like character piece without stylistic ties to folk ballads or to dramatic settings of poetic ballads (Ex. 2.8). This trend progressed to the so-called salon ballades by James Parakilas (p. 135) which are characterized by the operatic tradition—sweet melodies, plain accompaniments, and simple forms (usually ternary or variation forms). The ballades of Louis Moreau Gottschalk (1829-1869) are the most well-known among this type of ballades. They have a song-like quality with dance-like rhythms. For example, his final three ballades, published posthumously, were written in mazurka rhythms, and the Eighth Ballade (Ex. 2.9) has a theme resembling waltz.

Brahms's four ballades are distinctive among other lyrical ballades. They have qualities in common as a set. They are shorter than Chopin's ballades—nothing the same as the large-scale virtuoso productions of Chopin, even though the inspiration of tragic poems may be found in the works of both composers. Brahms' ballades are ternary in form, but with more flexibility in the relationships of the sections. They are more serious in character than salon ballades. The first ballade was related to the Scotch folk ballad "Edward" in Percy's *Reliques* (1756), published and translated by Herder in his influential collection of folk poetry (1778-1779). In this ballade (Ex. 2.10), Brahms created a new approach to a poetic model in which one can actually put words of the poem he cited (Herder's translation) in his music, as we can see the example of the opening theme of this ballade:

Dein Schaert, wie ists von Blut so roth?   "Why dois your brand sae drap wi' bluid,
Edward, Edward!   Edward, Edward?
Dien Schwert, wie ists von Blut so roth?   Why dois your brand sae drap wi' bluid?

Und gehst so traurig her?—O!
O ich hab geschlagen meinen Geyer todt,
Mutter, Mutter!
O ich hab geschlagen meinen Geyer todt,
Und keinen hab ich wie Er—O!

And why sae sad gang yee, O?"
"O, I hae killed my hauke sae guid,
Mither, mither,
O, I hae killed my hauke sae guid,
And I had nae mair bot hee, O."[6]

Ex. 2.8 Wieck Ballade

---

[6] This is the original English text of the opening stanza of "Edward". See Albert Friedman, *The Penguin Book of Folk Ballads of the English-Speaking World*. Harmondsworth, England: Penguin Book, 1976, p. 156.

36

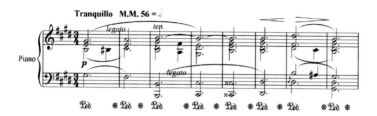

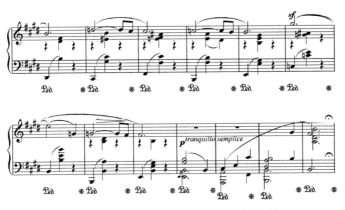

Ex. 2.9 Gottschalk Ballade Op. 90

Ex. 2.10 Brahms Ballade op. 10 no. 1

Not only is the way in which the melody fits the words strikingly, but more so is the way the gesture of that melody fits the tone of the voices in the poem. The poem is full of dialogues; each of the stanzas contains the questions of the mother and the replies of the son. Brahms presents two stanzas in the structure of the question-reply relationship—the music of each question and reply were demonstrated in the tempos of *Andante* and *Poco piu moto*. In the second stanza the music is a continuation of the first but with new cadences at the end, in which the bass of the second line becomes the melody. This device of a stanza that changes in the course of literal repetition is utilized similarly in Chopin's ballades. Rather than by

38

variation or embellishment, the treatment of the repetition of themes in Brahms' case is closer to that of the earlier German ballad-lieder.

On the other hand, the other three works of Op. 10 are not related to literature. The schemes applied in them resemble the common character pieces: ternary form, (No. 3), binary form (No. 4), and an arrangement of one main section with two episodes and a coda (No. 2) (Kirby, p. 237). In addition, the third ballade, constructed in a scherzo form with a lyrical trio, is far from the ballade genre, as shown by its "Intermezzo" title. Although it is not modeled on a poem or a song, the texture of the middle section—a homophonic texture of choral singing—recalls the opening of the first ballade "Edward". Brahms was credited with creating a new piano ballade cycle in his ballades Op. 10. The cycle is formed by musical relationships; the four ballades are stylistically and tonally connected, as well as being related in character and form. They are not analogous to different episodes sharing one single story, but more to a set of songs or poems written by one poet.

Throughout the entire nineteenth century, the arrangement of folk songs for piano was a large and varied project. Folk songs, or popular airs, were used frequently along with opera melodies and dance tunes in piano variations, rondos, and fantasies. Composers would record tunes and folklores from the places they traveled and subsequently arrange them into piano works. Glinka's *The Finnish Song* and Liszt's *Glanes de Woronince* are among the good examples. Glinka discovered and transcribed the tune when he visited Finland, and arranged and re-harmonized it for piano; but unfortunately he didn't record the words of it. *Glanes de Woronince* is a collection that Liszt reported what he heard from musicians, some of them Gypsies, near Woronince, a Ukrainian region of Podolia. The tribute of this set gives a strong emphasis of the nationalistic spirit from a collection of Ukrainian, Gypsy, and Polish sources by employing national airs to praise the national heroes.

In 1896 Julius Röntgen published his orchestral ballade *Ballade for Orchestra on a Norwegian Folk Melody*. It is a ballade comprised of a set of variations which inspired Grieg to compose a piano ballade in the form of variations. Unlike the ballades of Chopin, Liszt, and Brahms, Grieg's ballade is based on a Norwegian folk song, *Den nordlandske bondestand* which he presents in fourteen variations. The words were written by Kristine Aas and the song was found in Lindeman's collection *Aeldre og nyere norske Fjeldmelodier (Older and Newer Norwegisn Mountain Melodies)* (Ex. 2.11). Grieg's ballade took a further arrangement for the tune. First of all, his harmonization is very different from Linderman's; he used an incredibly chromatic descending bass line and a greater variety of chords connected chromatically in the inner parts. He also carried the momentum of the music by giving interesting cadences—the first half of the opening theme ends with a model cadence with a held bass on F while the top three voices sit on the G minor chord. The final cadence presents a strong effect of a major second in the inner voice (Ex. 2.12). Furthermore, Grieg broke free from the structure of the theme in the variations. Materials from keys, harmonies, rhythms, phrase-structures were subject to novel alternations for different characters. Indeed, Grieg's ballade, instead of a narrative work, is a variation set in which the later variations don't adhere to the original structure of the theme; in this sense, Grieg's idea of variations might stem from Beethoven's. Nevertheless, by choosing a folk song of his own country, Grieg gave a rich variety of arrangements to win attraction from other European's cultures in a contemporary way while being faithful to the tradition of his own country. In other words, his response to this work is similar to Chopin's response to his ballades, although the compositional strategy Grieg chose for his response is different from Chopin's.

Grieg's contemporary, Gabriel Fauré, published his Ballade Op. 19 in 1880, which was the composer's largest and finest early work for piano. Fauré, less involved with the Germanic tradition, followed the example of Chopin. He wrote character pieces for piano in the genres that Chopin used to master—barcarolles and nocturnes, thirteen of each, five impromptus, four waltz-caprices, a set of nine preludes, and a single mazurka. The ballade, which he later arranged for piano and orchestra, played an important role in the development of his musical creativity, and traced back to the influence of the first master of the piano ballade, Chopin. Additionally, the later arrangement for solo piano and orchestra began a new form of the ballade genre—concerto ballades, which became a crucial part of ballade repertory in the twentieth century.

40

Ex. 2.11 Norwegian folk song *Den nordlandske bondestand*

Ex. 2.12 Grieg's ballade

F. E. Kirby briefly concludes the development of French music with the competition with other musical styles:

In the seventeenth and eighteenth centuries French musicians waged heated battles regarding the relative merits of Italian music and musicians as opposed to their own. But in the later eighteenth and nineteenth centuries France's great musical rival became Germany; even though Italian opera remained capable of stimulating controversy, the new Germanic art of instrumental music clearly got the most attention. In the field of piano music additional influences came from Chopin and Liszt. (Kirby, p. 252)

From 1880 to 1903, when Wagner encouraged the incitement of Romanticism in music, composers in France and Russia led a revolution in terms of musical forms, orchestration, and styles, to build up a nature of aesthetic that differed from the Germanic Romanticism accomplished by Wagner. These composers, including Emmanuel Chabrier and Modest Petrovich Musorgsky, explored a new path of Impressionism. Among those creative composers, Fauré, Claude Debussy, Maurice Ravel, and Igor Stravinsky were the four most vital figures that directed the stage of contemporary music in the twentieth century.

The uniqueness of French contemporary style may be observed in the music of Fauré's ballade. This work has three main parts, and each of them carries one principal theme. The first part begins with an *Andante cantabile* in 4/4 time, and the theme, in F-sharp major, is sweet and lyrical as in other Fauré's piano works:

Ex. 2.13 The opening of Faure's ballade

After an enharmonic key change, the second theme is introduced in *Allegro moderato* in E-flat minor, the relative minor, and this theme often interacts with the first theme. The second part flows into a so-called *trait d'alliance* passage. This link passage, as James Parakilas describes, brings in a theme which dominates the rest of the work. This theme is first introduced by *Andante* in the meter of 6/8:

Ex. 2.14 The theme introduced in the Andante section of Faure's ballade

Later the *Allegro* version of this theme comes back to 4/4 time in B major and leads back to F-sharp major where the second and the third theme are developed together. Finally, the piece becomes one. Although the three parts manage different themes, the composer constructed a continuous process of thematic interaction and evolution among them. The relationship of themes reminds us of a stronger link to Chopin's barcarolle instead of Chopin's or Liszt's ballades in which the themes are opposed to each other. The growth of each thematic section in Fauré's ballade is gradual instead of dramatic or contrasting as in Chopin's and Liszt's ballades. In this sense, Fauré's ballade is distinguished from the earlier ballade tradition.

Both harmonically and melodically this ballade initiates a new style. The alternation of unrelated keys and chords is a new musical mean that for the future Impressionists. The themes, in general, are song-like with wavy accompaniments, and the swinging of two adjacent notes makes a perfect connection to bird songs. The thematic evolution with naturalistic tone-painting lets us consider this ballade as a musical discourse on the subject of nature, which Debussy developed even further than Fauré. According to a remark reported by Alfred Cortot, the ballade was an impression of nature influenced by the "Forest Murmurs" passage in Wagner's *Siegfried* (Auclert, p. 4). The effects of bird calls, leaf trembling, and the wavy accompaniment in the ballade link it to the spirit of traditional ballades, a juxtaposition between song and nature—the origin of folk songs.

The orchestral ballades in the nineteen century seemed to trace particular ballad stories; however, composers of piano ballades seldom took this approach. Chopin was observed to write his ballades according to the ballads of the particular poet. Other composers, like Liszt, and later Brahms, Grieg, and Faure barely followed a particular ballad model. Yet, there are few piano ballades that are modeled on particular ballads, although it is striking that they are not known in the primary repertory of the piano ballades. One of the earliest piano ballades associated with a particular poetic model was written by Julian Fontana (1810-1865), a friend of Chopin in Warsaw. The piece is titled "Ballade", but it includes a couple lines of a French version of Bürger's *Die Entführung*, which was published in 1778. Theordor Kullak (1818-1882) wrote his Ballade Op. 81, based on Bürger's ballad, under the name of "Lénore". The Russian pianist and composer Anton Rubinstein (1829-1894) used the same poem for his Ballade Op. 93. "The Ghost Ship,"[7] by Carl Tausig (1841-1871), was based on "Das Geisterschiff" by Moritz von Strachwitz, and is connected to the Nordic ballad settings and supernatural subjects. However, unlike other folk ballads, the story is narrated in the first person—an encounter with a ghost-cursed Viking ship in the storm of the North Sea. The story was possibly inspired by the ballad-like Flying Dutchman legend, either by Heine's story or Wagner's opera (Parakilas, p. 128).

To sum up, the piano ballades based on particular stories vary in poetic models, narrative styles, and musical forms. Yet, there is one thing in common: the composers didn't

---

[7] Tausig composed "The Ghost Ship" in both the orchestral and piano versions.

treat their ballades as a song or narrating voice, but their works focus on illustrating actions and settings, like storms, riding a horse, etc. The metaphor of these ballades is much similar to the most programmatic music in the nineteenth century.

CHAPTER III

MICKIEWICZ AND CHOPIN

In the report to Jeanquirit in Augsburg on the last art historians' ball of the editor of *Musical Time,* Schumann mentioned:

"I recollected very well that when Chopin played the ballade here,...at that time he also mentioned that certain poems of Mickiewicz had suggested his ballade to him. On the other hand, a poet might easily be inspired to find words to his music; it stirs one profoundly". (*On Music and Musicians*, p. 143)

Schumann's words show that Chopin's ballades were composed under the influence of Mickiewicz. In fact, according to his letters, Chopin had known about Mickiewicz' works since teenager, and later they both met in Paris. According to Chopin's letters and other documents regarding the lives of these two artists, Chopin's four ballades were created by the influence of Mickiewicz's ballads, as well as by Chopin's love of the country and the tradition of Polish language and narrative style. Mickiewicz published his ballads in his first book *Ballads and Romances* in 1822 in which he initiated Polish Romanticism. He wrote 2 or 3 ballads while in Russia (1824-1829) (*Trzech Budrysów* among them). He did not write any ballads while in exile. The message of the ballads is anti-classical, or anti-pseudo-classical. In addition, Mickiewicz's source came from the local mythology, and that it was typical to Romanticism northern mythology.

Chopin, on the other hand, was a pianist and composer with a taste of Polish poetic to the Europeans' eyes. His music is full of elegance, melancholy, and lyricism that was not only influenced in general by the Romanticism in Europe but also by the characteristics of Polish poetry, especially Mickiewicz's ballads and narrative poems. In 1831, Chopin wrote the first ballade, the year that he settled down in Paris. The melancholy in Chopin's music reflects his loneliness after he became an alien in France. Throughout his life in France, he never felt settled or accepted but, rather, abandoned and lost; happiness was nowhere to be found in his heart. Having the similar background as a Pole and an immigrant in foreign countries, Chopin seemed to resonate with the deep emotions implied in Mickiewicz's poems, thus transforming them into music. Therefore, as foreigners, the same pain was marked in the lives of both Mickiewicz and Chopin, and apparently was evoked in their works.

Life of Mickiewicz

The leader of Polish Romanticism, Adam Mickiewicz, was born at a time when Romanticism dominated, during the nineteenth-century literary movement in Europe. His best-known works include *Forefathers' Eve, Konrad Wallenrod, Grazyna*, as well as the long narrative poem *Pan Tadeusz*. The golden years of his writing career were during his exile in Russia; after his release he moved to Western Europe and became a spiritual leader for Polish emigrants.

Mickiewicz was born in Nowogródek, in the former grand duchy of Lithuania, on Christmas Eve, 1798. Nowogródek was the capital of one of the eleven palatinates in Lithuania. The Lithuanian state was formed in the late Middle Ages, and the majority of its population was Orthodox, speaking an East Slavic language. By the end of the fourteenth century, Lithuania was absorbed into Poland. By the first half of the seventeenth century, the upper strata of the country became Polonized and Catholic, people who were attracted by the political liberties and the highly cultured level of the Polish nobility, while the Uniate or Orthodox peoples maintained their own culture and language (Weintraub, p. 1).

During the childhood of Mickiewicz, the political environment had changed greatly in Poland and Lithuania. Three years before he was born, the lands of Poland were divided into three forces by Prussia, Austro-Hungry, and Russia. Prussian, which was unfriendly to the Poles, ruled the far western area of Poland, in which there was a modernized social structure; the eastern area of Poland, including the former Grand Duchy of Lithuania, was controlled by Tsarist Russia. Under the control of foreign forces, the progressive Poles gave hope to France and the army of Napoleon. In 1807 after his victory over Prussia, Napoleon established the so-called Duchy of Warsaw, including the territories occupied by Prussia and part of Central Poland containing Warsaw. In 1815, after Napoleon lost its war with Russia, the Congress of Vienna created a new Polish State—the Kingdom of Poland, which was bound with Russia—in which the Russian Tsar was the King of Poland. However, Lithuania simply became a part of Russian Empire. People in Lithuania still retained their traditions of living, and the influence of the Russian authority was not very significant. The national consciousness of the Lithuanian masses was still awakening.

Adam Mickiewicz grew up in an impoverished family. His father, Mikołaj Mickiewicz, was a small lawyer; he was a primitive, brutal and greedy man, and Adam never mentioned his father, who died early in 1812 (Weintraub, p. 11).

Adam's mother, Barbara Mickiewicz[1] also came from the petty gentry. Mikołaj and Barbara had five sons, and Mikołaj had a farm in Zaosie, about thirty miles south of Nowogródek. Adam studied in a local Dominican school, where the courses were traditional—most of them related to Latin.

Under the influence of Prince Adam Czartoryski, a personal friend of Tsar Alexander, University of Wilno became one of the most important educational centers in the lands of Poland in the nineteenth century. Mickiewicz studied at the University of Wilno from 1815 through 1819. During his time at Wilno, a young professor of history, Joachim Lelewel, was influential for young students because of his new ideas on medieval history and deep dedication to politics. He even had some connections with secret political societies, and his passion for history and politics deeply attracted the youth of the school. In addition, G. E. Groddeck, a German philologist, brought up the interest of Latin literature to Mickiewicz at a young age. Twenty years after his graduation Mickiewicz took the chair of Latin literature in the Academy of Lausanne.

Mickiewicz's early interest in his writing was the French Enlightenment from the philosopher Voltaire. Polish literature was strongly influenced in that period by the French Enlightenment. Among the poets he read during that period were Kochanowski, Krasicki, and Trembecki, who were the Polish poets of the Renaissance and the Enlightenment. However, soon after he started to teach in Kaunas in 1819 to 1823, his taste changed to the admiration of Romanticism, including the writers Schiller and Byron. Those years following his discovery of Romantic poetry, especially of Byron, were ones of widening of intellectual horizons and spiritual maturing. Mickiewicz was captured by Byron's spirit of revolution and individualism. Byron created his own cult of personality, the so-called Byronic hero—a defiant, melancholy young man, with a mysterious, unforgivable past. In his works, Byron usually glorified proud heroes, who always overcome their hardships. The concept of the Byronic hero had a tremendous influence on poetry, drama, music, novel, opera, and painting in nineteenth-century Europe. Mickiewicz was not the exception; as Weinstraub said, "Byron became for Mickiewicz the model of a modern poet-fighter for freedom" (Weintraub, p. 16). His most important work under Byron's influence was *Konrad Wallenrod*.

When he was in Wilno, Mickiewicz took part in a semisecret group known as the Philomaths and Philarets. The group was established in 1818, as a literary and scholarly

---

[1] Some scholars believe that Barbara was probably of Jewish origin. However, according to Wiktor Weintraub, the Jewish origin of Mickiewicz's mother side seems to be improbable. See Wiktor Weintraub, *The Poetry of Adam Mickiewicz*, p. 11.

association. Mickiewicz was a founding member, and the members of the group had serious intellectual interests, mostly in the field of literature. They met regularly, discussing their own literary works or other literary and critical works, both Polish and foreign. The cultural atmosphere of the Philomaths was the same as that of Wilno, the Enlightenment. Most of the literature they dealt with was Classical; the members believed in Reason, Rationalism, and the liberty of Mankind as their final goal. Although the Philomaths didn't have clear political purposes, their gatherings undoubtedly led the young students in progressive and patriotic directions.

While at the University of Wilno, Mickiewicz began to write poems in the classical style, adhering to the literary fashion at that time. However, because the classical forms hardly matched the new thoughts of Romanticism derived from the new movement in Western Europe, Mickiewicz and his colleagues began to consider the liberal and national spirits as a break out for the new style. He started to write romantic ballads, using the subjects from traditional folk songs and legends that he was familiar with in his childhood. His simple but powerful poetic language in his first volume of poetry, *Ballads and Romances*, published in 1822, became a turning point in the history of Polish literature. The book included ballads and romances with topics of lost love, and a preface about Romanticism occurring in Western Europe. *Ballads and Romances* initiated the Polish Romanticism, and soon brought him fame. Later, in the next year, he wrote *Grasyna*, a tale in verse, and two parts of the romantic drama, *Forefathers' Eve*.

Forefathers' Eve was the name of a ceremony in memory of the ancestors among the common folk in many parts of Lithuania, Prussia and Courland. The second part deals with the theme of earthy suffering. It describes the apparitions of ill-treated tenants—the unresolved spirits of two children who cannot enjoy the joy of Heaven owing to their inexperience of sorrow, and the unanswered spirit of a village girl who never tasted love and grief. The fourth part takes place on All Souls' Day; this is a monodrama about the confession of a young suicide victim, who suffered insanity and death. The third part, however, was completed after he left Russia, in 1832. This part is comparatively more complex, enigmatic, and longer than other parts.

In 1823 Mickiewicz returned to Wilno and prepared his third volume of poetry. However, the Russian authorities suddenly detected the Philomaths, which they considered an anti-Russian organization. Mickiewicz and his friends were imprisoned and after a long investigation, Mickiewicz was sentenced to exile in Russia. On October 22, 1824, he received his orders to leave Lithuania, and after negotiating with the Russian government, he finally was sent to St. Petersburg. He left his home country on October 25, 1824, never to return.

During his exile in Russia, he was befriended by many leading Russian writers, including Aleksandr Pushkin. In 1828 he published his most famous epic poem *Konrad Wallenrod*. The theme of this epic is about a Lithuanian master who fights for the independence of his country under the Teutonic order. Konrad Wallenrod is a typical Byronic hero standing out for a national struggle—a Teutonic knight, finally discovered as a Lithuanian, is kidnapped by Teutonic Knights when he was a child. His past is not implied until the fourth canto "The Banquet"; in this canto Mickiewicz interrupts the bard's song "Tale" and tells the audience how a Lithuanian child named Walter was kidnapped by the Teutonics and was brought up with the name of Alf. Alf-Walter fled the Knights and took refuge in the Lithuanian town of Kowno. This is the section where Mickiewicz uses unrhymed hexameters, a new technique in Polish poetry.

After the bard's song, Wallenrod was moved and began to sing. This is the ballad "Alpuhara" about a crusade of Spain: the last king of the Moors, Almanzor, defended the town of Alpuhara from the Spaniards. This ballad, like the bard's song "Tale," implies a theme of heroic self-sacrifice for the good of the homeland (Welsh, p. 69). Finally, in the fifth canto, Wallenrod was found to be a betrayer of the Teutonics. At the end he was reunited with his long-lost wife, Aldona, whom he met in Kowno; he asked her to escape but she refused. Finally Wallenrod drank a cup of poison, and simultaneously Aldona killed herself in the tower. The plot of *Konrad Wallenrod* portrayed not only a tragedy between two great lovers who were separated by the historical circumstances, but also a product of hurt national feelings by Russian persecutions—imprisonment, trial, and exile (Weintraub, p. 125). As both Weintraub and Welsh quoted from Machiavelli, "You must know there are two ways of fighting—a man must be both wolf and lion" (Weintraub, p. 123; Welsh, pp. 64-65), Konrad Wallenrod, a hero created by Mickiewicz, has the qualities of both wolf—with cunning and treachery—and lion—with strength and courage. Mickiewicz used a medieval myth to imply his political revenge.

In 1829 Mickiewicz left Russia and went to Germany, where he visited Goethe in Weimar. He also went to Bohemia, Switzerland, and Rome. In Rome he lived in an international society, a place where Polish, Russian, French, and American artists gathered. In 1830, the Polish-Russian uprising began. Mickiewicz left Italy in 1831 and tried to join the insurrection which came to nothing. However, this was a crucial moment of Mickiewicz's life, when he saw the beaten Polish army crossing the Prussian border and witnessed the horror of the war. Later, he went to Dresden, visited the refugees and used their hard fate as material in the third part of *Forefathers' Eve*. It was published in 1832, and eventually Mickiewicz was marked not only a romantic poet but also a poet "serving the public cause" (Kridl, p. 9). Part III takes its place within the framework of the whole drama as a synthesis of poetry, music, and gesture—elements dear to the Romantic spirit (Welsh, p. 72). It has its own gods, its own mortal laws, and its own mythological system. The most significant goal of Romanticism is that the writer creates his own myth. Indeed, Mickiewicz decided to portray his own personal tragedy and, by using the elements of dramatic functions, to eternalize it. After biblical paragraphs from the tenth chapter of the Gospel of Matthew, the scene shows a prisoner asleep in his cell, like Byron's prisoner of Chillon, which symbolizes a patriotic Pole. This depicted the political tragedy of Poland and presented a vision for the future, in which this country needs redemption from the Will of God. Tormented by the self-reproved in the national struggle, Mickiewicz suffered the powerlessness of fighting for his own nation and the loneliness of being an emigrant in foreign countries:

> Fair words and fairer thoughts are mine;
> Much do I feel, writing early and late;
> My soul like a widow's must still repine—
> To whom my songs shall I dedicate?
>
> To thoughts and words I give birth each day—
> Why do they not my sorrow appease?
> Because my soul is a widow gray
> And only many orphans see.
>
> Winter and spring will pass away,
> Fair weather will pass as the storms are blown;
> But grief in the pilgrim's heart will stay,
> For he is a widower and alone.[2]

Finally he settled down in Paris. In 1832 he published *The Books of Polish Nation and of the Polish Pilgrimage* and *Pan Tadeusz* in 1834. By that time the mass of emigrants from Poland considered him as a national poet. The insurrection in 1831 encouraged him to introduce a new view toward the redemption of mankind. He named the Poles as the "chosen people"; through Poland's sufferings Europe would be reborn, and the revolution of Poland

---

[2] From *The Pilgrim's Song* by Adam Mickiewicz, written in 1832, translated by George Rapall Noyes, 1944.

would lead the world to universal freedom (Weintraub, p. 151). Mickiewicz used the doctrines of the Polish Messianism to elevate the pride and to raise the hopes of the Polish people, especially Polish emigrants. Through the emotional strength and poetic beauty in works like *Forefathers' Eve, Part III* and *The Books of Polish Nation and of the Polish Pilgrimage*, Mickiewicz spoke to his suffering people (Noyes, p. 38).

Pan Tadeusz expressed Mickiewicz's longing for his homeland. It is a humorous epic and recounts the quarrel between two noble families. It contains colors and richness in movement and sound to demonstrate an idyllic world of Lithuania. The characters in this epic, recognized as typical characters of the old Polish gentry, have qualities of goodness and happiness greater than any "real people" we might expect. The ancient look of the setting and the simple-hearted characters depicted Mickiewicz's desire for going back to where he used to live in his childhood. Yet, this epic became a channel for the poet not only to express his homesickness, but also to capture the hearts of the whole Polish people, from the peasant children to the literary specialists. Mickiewicz's ambition described in the epilogue of *Pan Tadeusz* has been fulfilled: "Oh, if some time I might attain this joy—that this book might find shelter beneath roofs of thatch, and that the village girls…might take into their hands this book, simple as their songs!" (Noyes, p. 40)

Pan Tadeusz is regarded as a monument of Polish national literature. Fryderyk Chopin, the greatest composer, composed the "Revolution" etude three years before the epic was written. Chopin's ballades kept the same charm and fire, typical in Mickiewicz's poems, and his polonaises were also viewed as a sort of respect in the national manifestation.

After writing *Pan Tadeusz*, Mickiewicz practically concluded his career as a poet. For the remainder of his life, Mickiewicz was a professor, a journalist, a religious and social worker. Soon after he published *Pan Tadeusz* he married Celina Szymanowska, but their marriage was unhappy. During his period of teaching at the College de France (1840-1844) he was enthusiastic about the doctrines of mysticism under the influence of Andrzej Towianski (1799-1878), but later in 1947 the relationship was broken. This event caused him to be relieved of his teaching job in the College. In 1848 he went to Rome to organize a Polish armed force against Austria for the liberation of Italy. After the outbreak of the Crimean War, he went to Turkey to raise Polish armies in Turkey to fight against Tsarist Russia. On November 26, 1855, he died during a cholera epidemic in Constantinople. The life of a passionate poet, fighting for the freedom of his country, ended.

Life of Chopin

In 1831, Robert Schumann wrote an article for the leading German musical periodical, the Allgemeine musikalische Zeitung, to introduce the then-unknown Chopin to the German public. He made one of the most famous critical comments in music history on Chopin's variations for the piano Op. 2 based on the theme of Mozart's "Lá ci darem la mano" from Don Giovanni: "Hats off, gentlemen, a genius!" Schumann was amazed by Chopin's well-written early composition as he compared the variations with Beethoven's and Schubert's. He concluded: "I nevertheless bow to his genius, his aspiration, his mastery!"

This evidence demonstrates Schumann's admiration for Chopin's genius and maturity as a composer since he was a teenager. His early music, influenced by Hummel and Field, is affected with charm and sweetness. Chopin's music is full of poetic flavor—beautiful melody, rich harmony, and dramatic atmosphere. His growth, as he spent most of his life in foreign countries, directs his music toward multiple dimensions and colors to depict the reflection of mourning on his lonely life and the pity toward his home country's political tragedy. His passion is mature, well-sustained within an organized and elaborate form, and with the passion vibratant in his music, decorated by harmonic complexity and melodic layers—yet the dark and melancholy motive is never lost. He made Bach served as his chief model, and within the fabric of strange and chromatic harmonies, a soul of madness sang through his favorite instrument—the piano that was never sung as such in history. The reflection of patriotism in his music has made Chopin recognized as the musical soul of Poland. He became the open door to the West because he inducted the musical ideas, harmonies and rhythms of Eastern/Slavic to the Western Europeans.

Fryderyk Chopin was born in Żelazowa Wola, twenty-eight miles from Warsaw, in 1810[3], the second son of French teacher Nicolas Chopin who played the flute and the piano. Nicolas was born in Lorraine in the northeastern France, and immigrated to Warsaw in 1787. He never returned to France, just as his son, Fryderyk, never returned to Poland after he moved to France. Fryderyk's mother, Justyna Krzyżanowska Chopin, was born of a well-educated Polish family. His mother was ideal, as George Sand declared, Chopin's "only love" (Huneker, p. 6). Seven months after Fryderyk was born, Nicolas decided to move to Warsaw for good and there he accepted a teaching position at the Warsaw Lyceum. Fryderyk grew up in an intelligent and lovely family with a well-educated French father and an adoring Polish mother. He was happy and home-loved in his childhood.

---

[3] The date of Chopin's birth now is believed to have been either March 1, 1810 (according to his statement in 1833) or February 22, 1810 as on his birth certificate. See Huneker, p. 4.

During Chopin's childhood, Poland was ruled as a kingdom under the control of Tsar Alexander I of Russia and his brother, Archduke Konstanty. Warsaw was a sophisticated cultural capital of Eastern Europe. It had a national theater for operas, three concert halls, churches, and private homes for concerts. Owing to an increase of the rich aristocratic and bourgeois population, every decent family had a piano and at least one person could play it. Additionally, Warsaw had literary periodicals, mostly discussing works of the romantics, as well as a musical one weekly. Because of the huge demand of the musical population, Polish and foreign composers were willing to publish their music through Warsaw's publishers. Therefore, nurtured in the active musical environment, the Chopins naturally had a piano and their parents often played the piano, violin, or flute with each other. When Fryderyk was three or four years old, he started to learn the piano from his mother; soon by the age of six he had already mastered the instrument very quickly. He taught himself to improvise and harmonize all the melodies he had ever heard, but his parents concluded that he needed to have serious and systematic education on the piano and theory.

Chopin's first serious teacher was Wojciech Żywny. He was a sixty-year-old violinist and music teacher from Bohemia. Mr. Żywny taught the young Chopin composition and piano, and he recognized Chopin's unusual talent, trying to guide and nurture his musical maturity. The most important contribution Żywny made was that he introduced the music of Johann Sebastian Bach to the young Chopin, engendering inspiration and love for it. Żywny asked the young Chopin to practice Bach's *Well-Tempered Clavier* on a daily basis, and Chopin followed it with a religious obedience. It is not surprising that Chopin wrote his twenty-four preludes under the influence of Bach's own forty-eight preludes and fugues. He appreciated Żywny's teaching and inspiration which influenced Chopin's compositional career, as he said when he was in the tour of Vienna at the age of nineteen:

All the professional musicians are captivated with my Rondo. Beginning with Kapellmeister Lachner and ending with the piano-tuner, they are surprised at the beauty of the composition. I know that both ladies and artists liked me...Shappansigh reminded me yesterday that, as I am leaving Vienna so soon, I must also come back soon. I replied that I shall come to learn; to which the baron retorted:—"In that case you have nothing to come for." Only compliments, but pleasant ones. No one here wants to take me as a pupil. Blahetka said nothing surprised him so much as my having learned all that in Warsaw. I answered that under Żywny and Elsner the greatest donkey could learn. (*Chopin's Letters*, p. 57)

The Bach influence may explain why Chopin's music seemed to sound closer to Baroque masters than that of his contemporaries. Chopin became a bridge between two epochs—between Beethoven, who had died when Chopin was seventeen, and of course Bach, as an ancestor of the Romantics, and a model for Mozart and Beethoven (Szulc, p. 33).

At very early ages Chopin showed his talent in piano playing. He made his first public performance as a pianist in February 1818, a week before his eighth birthday. His fame spread quickly and he was allowed to play for royal families such as the Archduke Konstanty family, Empress Maria Feodorova, and the Tsar Alexander. However, Chopin performed only seven times in public before his first trip to Vienna in 1829. In fact Chopin did not enjoy playing before large audiences. He had only thirty concerts in his lifetime—the least publicly heard among the important pianists of his generation. Perhaps psychologically he was shy and did not enjoy playing before concert hall audiences, which he often called "people I don't know" in letters to his best friends. Another consideration, which is purely a musical one, is that Chopin's playing was sensitive in touch and color, and it was perfectly suited for salons and small private rooms. During his permanent stay in Paris, Chopin always felt comfortable and confident playing in salons and private homes surrounded by his artist-friends.

To assure a better musical education for his son, Mikołaj decided to send the young Chopin to Józef Elsner, a fifty-two-year-old Silesian German composer and director of newly built Warsaw Conservatory. Elsner taught the young man that counterpoint and harmony can refine his compositional skill to a higher level. Chopin took private composition lessons with Elsner for three years, and later at the age of sixteen he entered a three-year program at the Central Music School—part of the Warsaw Conservatory. Under Elsner's tutoring Chopin soon established his own compositional style—mastering beautiful counterpoint, harmonic voicing, and melodies. His extraordinary sensitivity for the sonority of the piano enabled him to manage complex melodic and harmonic relationships; even unpredictable discords would sound musically coherent.

During his teenage in Poland, Chopin had opportunities to hear plenty of folk dance music and songs—polonaises, mazurkas, krakowiaks, obereks, and the Jewish country music while he spent vacations in Polish countryside. At the same time Chopin experienced the virtuoso violin playing of Paganini, the great singing of Angelica Catalani and Henrietta Sonntag, and the piano performances of Johann Nepomuk Hummel. In his trip to Berlin, he heard George Frideric Handel's *Messiah*; in Vienna, he saw Rossini and Meyerbeer operas. Chopin always adored human voices and loved songs and operas; hence the melodies of his music possess the beauty of vocal style. In Dresden, Chopin was impressed by the dramatic performance of Goethe's *Faust*. Without a doubt, Goethe, as the father of Romanticism in literature, had effects on music as well. Therefore, although the folk influence was great in his music, Chopin was a man of international taste and not just limitedly considered as a Polish composer. His music was a representation of romantic taste for his contemporaries and later generations.

In May 1829, Tsar Nicholas I became the ruler of Poland after the death of his father, Tsar Alexander. Unlike Alexander, Nicholas I had a reign of terror in Russia and Poland, and the young Poles, including Chopin and his friends, started to oppose the Russian rule, planting the seed of the civil rebellion that occurred in the following year. At this time, Chopin was busy writing new music, such as a new piano concerto, first mazurkas and waltzes, and polonaise in G-flat major. He often spent hours at Dziurka, a coffeehouse in Warsaw where artists, journalists, and aspiring politicians gathered to discuss the politics of Poland. Chopin met the young Polish poets with whom he composed patriotic songs in Paris in few years, such as Stefan Witwicki and Bohdan Zaleski. He also read poems of Adam Mickiewicz, which were to inspire the creation of his ballades later. Among his poet-friends they often talked about not only politics but also literature of Poland and Western Europe that initiated the Romanticism. He made friends with lawyers, music critics, pianist Maurycy Mochnacki, and newspaper editors; these were people secretly against Tsar Nicholas. Mochnacki became one of the political leaders of the Warsaw rebellion[4]. He immigrated to France during the Exile and kept the Polish flame growing with Chopin in Paris.

In November 1830, Chopin made his second international tour to Dresden, Prague, and Vienna, just few weeks after he left Warsaw the rebellion began. Hearing the news from Warsaw, Chopin suffered emotionally and physically, and his fragile health was exacerbated owing to his inner mourning concerning the collapse of his own country. The emotional and physical pain was described in his letter to Jan Matuszyński when he was in Vienna:

I was to have gone to hear Pasta; you know I have letters from the Saxon court to the Milan viceroy's wife. But how am I to go? My parents tell me to please myself, and I don't want to go. To Paris? Here they advise me to wait. Return home? Stay here?—Kill myself?—Not write to you? Give me some advice, what to do. Ask the persons who dominate me, and write me their opinion, and so it shall be. (*Chopin's Letters*, p. 132)

---

[4] A period while the Poles immigrated to other countries, mostly to France, owing to the Warsaw rebellion against Russians. Many of them were intellectuals like scientists, artists, and writers.

In the diary he kept during the fall of Warsaw he wrote:

Why do we live such a miserable life, which devours us and serves to make cadavers! The clocks on Stuttgart towers ring the nocturnal hour. Ah, how many cadavers were created in the world at that moment! Mothers of children—mothers (who) have lost children—how many plans erased...Ho much sadness from the cadavers at this moment and how much consolation...How many creatures suffocated by cadavers. Good and bad cadaver! Virtue and crime! So it is clear that death is the best act of man—but what will be the worst? Birth, as contrary to the best act. Thus I am right to be angry that I was brought into the world...I am not useful to people because I have no (leg) calves and no snouts...And even if I had them, I would not have anything else...Does the cadaver have calves? (Szulc, p. 47)

Chopin's personality disorders and visions of death gradually intensified with time. Additionally, his experiences of dark fantasies and illusions made him feel vulnerable; it was only in his music that he honestly opened his heart. His state of mind was written in a notebook, "And here I am, helpless. Here I am with my empty hands!" was reflected in his works such as the G minor Ballade, the D minor Prelude, and the "Revolutionary" Etude while he learned of the war in Poland (Jarecki, in *Frederick Chopin 1810-1849*, p. 35).

In 1831, Chopin decided to go to Paris. At this time, Paris was the capital for Romantics—as poets, musicians, and painters who visited there as their pilgrimage from other countries. Thousands of books, poems, and compositions were published, and concerts were performed frequently in Paris. Fundamentally, the 1789 revolution altered the social and political context. As the economy expanded, the bourgeoisie and the proletariat were growing immensely and believed that they had the power to control the society. They began to emerge as new potential political forces against the aristocratic class. In this environment Romanticism in the arts and literature was cultivated as a glorious ideal. Chopin was fortunate to catch the wave.

In Paris, Chopin's genius was recognized widely, owing to his personal charm and appearance, self-confidence as a musician, discipline, and hard work. He was praised by women and talented artists. But on the other hand, the anxiety arising from his inner loneliness and homesickness caused intense suffering of depression and rage. Nevertheless, his sense of humor, which probably covered up his fear, warmth, love, and sensitive nature, were the reasons that he socialized well with his new friends: Liszt, Mendelssohn, Vincenzo Bellini, Hector Berlioz, Irish pianist George Alexander Osborne, and the painter Delacroix. All the artists he befriended were of outstanding talent, and most were of his same generation. They often gathered at Café de Paris or some other fancy restaurants; naturally they criticized one another, especially when they became old men. However, it was a perfect group —the "Romantic generation" that had the same goal in structuring a "new style" replacing classicism. On occasions they judged one another bitterly, but subconsciously they were all influenced by one another. All of them represented different cultures and backgrounds— German, Italian, French, English, Hungarian, and Polish. Yet together they created a European style, which inspired the art of the nineteenth century.

In Paris Chopin joined other exiles to share their spiritual struggle and to dedicate their lives to Poland. Among them were his friends from Warsaw—Julian Fontana, Alexander Orłowski, the families of the Czartoryskis, the Platers, and the Wodzińskis. In a testimony to his feelings, in a letter of December 25, 1831 to Tytus Wojciechowski, Chopin wrote: "I am gay on the outside, especially among my own folk (I count Poles my own); but inside something gnaws at me" (*Chopin's Letters*, p. 166). His patriotism was revealed in his music as well as "in his choice of friends, in his preference for pupils, in the frequent and considerable services that he liked to render his compatriots" (Liszt, p. 119).

A great deal was made of Chopin's love affairs and they clearly played a major role in his life. Besides Delfina Potocka, with whom he maintained an intimate friendship throughout his life, there were three women who had an important influence on him: Konstancja Gladkowska, Maria Wodzinska, and Amandine Lucile Aurore Dudevant née Dupin—best known by her pen-name, George Sand. Konstancja Gladkowska was a talented singer and studied in the Warsaw Conservatory; Chopin's admiration of her occurred when he was nineteen and about to leave the country, but his love was curtailed after she married Joseph Grabowski. His second relationship with Maria Wodzinska was stronger and more serious than the first one. When Chopin left Poland she was a child. After the rebellion of Warsaw the Wodzinska's family moved out of Poland, and Chopin paid them for a trip to Dresden in 1835. At that time Chopin met Maria, who turned out to be a beautiful young lady, and fell in love with her. They spent time together in Dresden, and finally Chopin proposed to her and kept his promise with her mother that he would take care of his health. However, after Chopin came back to Paris, he was seriously ill, and his social functions were reduced due to his bad health. Maria eventually married Jozef Skarbek and Chopin fell into deep depression.

As he drowned his grief owing to the break with Maria, Chopin found a new source of inspiration in his friendship with George Sand. They first met through an invitation of Franz Liszt. George Sand adored Chopin's charm and talent. Their relationship began in 1838 and continued until 1846. The story of the "masculine" Sand and the "feminine" Chopin became one of the most well-known love affairs from the Romantic era. They lived together for eight years, a very fruitful life, and it is in this period that Chopin composed some of his best works. Sand was six years older than Chopin, and there is no doubt that her motherly instinct and strong character kept their relationship strong for as long as it lasted. Chopin was a sickly man, so Sand nursed him like a child and supplied the warmth and freedom for his life and career. She offered Chopin what he truly wanted in his heart—care, companionship, and security. In the winter of 1838-1839 Sand took Chopin to the island of Majorca and then to her country home in Nohant that summer.

However, their separation came gradually owing to family forces; the children of Sand were divided in two opposing groups with and against Chopin. In addition, Chopin's emotional instability widened the gap between the two lovers, and following their final accidental meeting on March 4, 1848, they were never to see each other again.

Chopin continued teaching privately in Paris to support himself financially even though his health was worsening. Not having been heard in public since 1842 his friends encouraged him to give a concert. On February 16, 1848, Chopin performed before a selected audience, which proved to be his last public appearance in Paris. Meanwhile his Scottish pupil Jane Stirling invited him to England. Although he was very ill, Chopin decided to go and even attended some social gatherings with royal families. He gave several concerts in London and Scotland, and met several important figures such as Dickens, Carlyle, Jenny Lind, and Emerson.

After he came back to Paris, Chopin struggled with his illness. Two days before he died, Delfina Potocka visited him and he asked her to sing for him for the last time, engendering the last touch of happiness in his life. Chopin passed away in the company of his sister Ludwika, Princess Czartoryska, and George Sand's daughter, Solange Clésinger. He was buried at Lachaise Cemetery in Paris, but he requested to have his heart kept in Warsaw, where it was finally interred in the Church of the Holy Cross in Warsaw.

Life Connections between Chopin and Mickiewicz

Although much has been discussed about Chopin's participation in Parisian salon life, it was in Warsaw's salons that the young Chopin made connections with the most talented artists in one of the important cultural capitals in Europe. Fortunately he was mature enough for intellectual discussions with elders and artistic peers and through the musical experiences in public concerts, which were the stimuli for his mind beyond the education he had received in the Conservatory. It is importantly recognized that the effect of Warsaw's salons played a profound role in Chopin's intellectual and musical development.

The salons in Warsaw resembled the salons of other European cities, and could usually be divided into three major categories: the social salon (which gathered family and friends to introduce newcomers and provide entertainment); the intellectual or literature salon (which was set up by a discussion club and sometimes devoted to a specific aesthetic agenda); and the musical salon (professional artists and amateurs gathered in musical performances) (Goldberg, p. 2). Typically, among the participants of intellectual and musical salons were mostly higher educated aristocrats, artists, University and Gymnasium professors, students and graduates, or free professionals. Chopin had close relationships with all of these circles, and his talent would allow him the privilege to mingle within these aristocratic salons.

Starting around 1815, a group of amateur literati, known as "the Society of Exes," gathered to read their works and theater reviews, which they published and signed "X." Their meetings were hosted mostly at the home of General Krasiński, after the lectures of Professor Osiński. During the years 1826-1828, Chopin attended Professor Osiński's lectures and remained during some afternoons for the discussions in the Society's meetings. The benefit for Chopin to join the lectures and the Society's meetings was to discover the older generation of writers and poets, scholars. The current literary issues discussed in these lectures and meetings interested the young Chopin. The debate of classical values and new ideas in the discussions opened Chopin's mind and senses, which affected his music tremendously.

Zofia Czartoryski, a member of the Society of Exes, and her husband Stanisław Kostka Zamoyski, often held literary salons in the Azure Palace, where they invited officials and professionals of the higher social class. This particular place also accommodated a number of outstanding young talents, and during the readings in their gatherings they discovered that the poems of Adam Mickiewicz were the most provocative of Romanticism (Goldberg, p. 4). Chopin was invited for the first time in childhood, and in later years, often visited. It is likely that Chopin was profoundly inspired by Mickiewicz's poems owing to the discussions in Zamoyskis' salons.

In the years before he moved away from Warsaw, Chopin had great opportunities to join both the side of the Gymnasium and University professors, artists, and poets of the older generation and the other side of the young poets and influential cultural thinkers. His close friends, Antoni Edward Odyniec, Stefan Witwicki, Bohdan Zaleski, and Count Zygmunt Krasiński (General Krasiński's son), were representatives of Romanticism in Polish literature.

At the time of Romantic awakening in literature, Chopin also sought new and free forms of expression from the inspiration of poetry, literature, folklore, and new aesthetic values from German and French Romanticism, which attracted the young generation. Mickiewicz, the greatest image of Polish Romanticism in literature, was the model for the young Chopin and his literary peers. Since the publication of the poem entitled *Romanticism* in 1821, which articulated the Romantic aesthetic in its words, the conflict between the Classical and Romantic Schools in Warsaw started to open up in public, and Mickiewicz became a visionary icon for young artists. Jan Sniadecki, one of the most important scientists at the University of Wilno, made a seminal statement against the Romantic movement in a Wilno newspaper:

"Poets now bring on the stage assemblies of witches with their incantations and charms, walking ghosts and vampires, dialogues of devils and angels and the like. What is there new and witty in all this? Every peasant woman has long been familiar with beauties such as these and speaks of them with a laugh of contempt. Can imbecility and folly, revived from ages of ignorance, credulity, and superstition, amuse and delight in the eighteenth and the nineteenth centuries even the vulgar throng—not to mention well-educated people?" ("Introduction", *Poems by Adam Mickiewicz*, Noyes, p. 6)

Mickiewicz felt the repugnance about Sniadecki's statement, the representative of rationalism of the eighteenth century, so that he replied in his *Romanticism* and noted that "feeling and faith" of a normal maid or the common people can reveal the truth more vividly than "eyes and spectacles" of learned people. The romantic poets, like Mickiewicz, valued the spirit world of mankind, and *Romanticism* directly evolved the innermost feelings of the common people. "Look in your heart, that still may see aright!" answered Sniadecki's questioning about the Romantic trend among the young poets. In addition, the significance of Romanticism—the capture of the heroic images and the supernatural forces, for example— provides a relief from the tragic political circumstances of enslaved Poland, and became a means of spiritual resolution for the young artists like Chopin and his peers during the exile in Paris.

Mickiewicz's *Ballads and Romances* (including *Romanticism*) was published in 1822. Chopin kept a copy of it as his possession since he was sixteen (Szulc, p. 52), and became an admirer of Mickiewicz's poems. He was attracted to Mickiewicz's concentration on folk values and the strata of verses. Soon after he composed songs to Mickiewicz's poems, as well as to other poets' works. It appears that Chopin wrote his songs with an inspired casuality—composing them when he was moved by a poem at any given moment. He also wrote songs for social occasions, like attending salons, or as a gift to his friends. Chopin neglected putting some of them on paper and never published his songs; but after his death, Julian Fontana, Chopin's schoolmate, published his sixteen songs in Warsaw and one later appeared in Berlin.[5] Chopin composed two highly expressive love songs to poems by Mickiewicz, and others to poems by Stefan Witwicki, Józef Bohdan Zaleski, and Count Zygmunt Krasiński. Simple in structure and sentiment, Chopin's songs brought a first-hand folkloric taste, a naïve tenderness, an intimate charm, a longing reflection, and deep underlying feelings for his country.

The other part of Chopin's repertoire most influenced by Mickiewicz was his four ballades. In 1831, Chopin wrote his own Ballade No. 1 in G minor, Op. 23, a new genre for piano. The four ballades are among Chopin's greatest musical achievements as a composer. Relayed by Schumann concerning the meaning of the ballades, Chopin mentioned that Mickiewicz's ballads had led him to this idea.

Chopin and Mickiewicz first met in 1832 and soon formed a warm friendship. Both of them belonged to the Polish Literary Society and other emigrant organizations. Mickiewicz was also once a guest in Chopin-Sand's salons, although Chopin's contacts with Mickiewicz were not limited to social occasions. George Sand admired his poetry and drama and aided in promoting his name in France with her 1839 *Essai sur le drame fantastique: Goethe, Byron et Mickiewicz (Essay on Fantastic Drama: Goethe, Byron, and Mickiewicz),* published in *Revue des deux mondes* (Szulc, p. 195). In 1840, Chopin attended some of Mickiewicz's lectures with Sand on Slavic Literature at the Collège de France, translating some of his poems for George Sand (Chomiński, p. 120, p. 132). He was also involved in arranging an improved translation of Mickiewicz's *Dziady (The Forefathers' Eve)* for Sand's article in *Essai sur le drame fantastique: Goethe, Byron et Mickiewicz.*[6]

According to Andrzej Walicki's statement, the Polish Romanticism of 1830s and 1840s was rooted in the philosophical expression of the Polish emigration, which is called the "Messianism—a belief in Poland as a Messiah of nations—their redeemer, whose sufferings would bring salvation and a new age for mankind" (Zakrzewska, p. 5):

---

[5] Besides the seventeen songs collected by Fontana, an eighteenth was published in 1912 titled "Enchantments". It probably was composed in 1847.
[6] It was indicated in a letter of March 27, 1839 to Grzymała for translating to French. See *Chopin's Letters*, p. 197.

Polish romantic Messianism was a product of a national catastrophe of 1831—of the defeat of the insurrection against Russia—and of the tragedy of the political emigration which followed. We may define it more general terms as a hope born out of despair; as a result of multiple deprivation; as an expression of an increased feeling of self-importance combined with a sense of enforced rootlessness and isolation in an alien world; as an ardent search for religious consolation combined with a bitter sense of having been let down by the traditional religious authority. (Walicki, p. 242)

Therefore, Messianism became a fundamental belief for Polish emigrants, having suffered through the national collapse and bringing hope and salvation to the world. In Mickiewicz's and Chopin's works this belief was articulated frequently: the melancholy and loneliness in their minds and feelings were expressed through their interests in folklore and national virtues. It exemplified the concept of nationalism, which is a part of the universal Romantic tradition, and provided hope for the future while they were isolated in foreign countries. This ideology of Messianism affected the lives and works of both Chopin and Mickiewicz, especially the character of Chopin's music, which was profoundly transformed after the events of the 1831 tragedy. In Chopin's Stuttgart diary, he wrote:

It was like some momentary death of feeling; for a moment I died in my heart; no, my heart died in me for a moment...Alone! Alone!—There are no words for my misery; how can I bear this feeling— (*Chopin's Letters*, p. 150)

Furthermore, Jeremy Siepmann observes:

The fall of Warsaw effected a sea change, not only in Chopin's perception of himself but of the world around him. It brought his consciousness of personal identity and his now consuming sense mission into sharper relief than ever before, and the change was soon reflected in his music. Above all, it gave him searingly intensified awareness of Poland and the centrality of his own, deep-rooted Polishness. (p. 81)

Mickiewicz's expression of homelessness and alienation in foreign lands was provocative in his drama *Dziady (Forefathers' Eve)* Part III through the struggle of Konrad, his alter ego hero, with God:

> Alone! Ah, men! And who of you, diving
> My spirit, grasps the meaning of its song?
> Whose eye will see the radiance of its shining?
> Alas, who toils to sing for men, toils long!

63

(*Poems by Adam Mickiewicz*, p. 270)

Mickiewicz also reacted to his daily experience in Paris with complaints and longing for his homeland. In the prologue of *Pan Tadeusz*, he wrote:

> To think of such things in a Paris street,
> Where on my ears the city's noises beat
> With lies and curses, and with plans ill-fated,
> And fiendish quarrels and regrets belated!
>
> Alas for us who fled in times of pest
> And, timid souls, took refuge in the west!
> Terror pursued wherever we might go,
> In every neighbor we discerned a foe;
> At last they bound us up in fetters tight,
> And bade us die as quickly as we might.
> (*Pan Tadeusz*, translated by Kenneth R. Mackenzie, p. 578)

Mickiewicz's life in exile was full of grief and burdens beyond his other fellow refugees. His wife began to have periodic mental breakdowns, and in addition he had to take care of their young children in addition to their mentally ill mother. Feeling exhausted because of the sufferings of his family and alienation, Mickiewicz yielded to his own fanaticism for a messianic religion founded by Andrezj Towianski, but unfortunately his pain couldn't be healed so easily—he ultimately lost his position in the Collège de France.

Both Chopin and Mickiewicz shared the source of similar life experiences: they lived in foreign lands and never went back to their home country after the 1831 collapse, and they both felt themselves to be a part of their compatriots' society even though they gained fame and respect among Parisians and others. Although they didn't belong to the Great Emigration in a strict sense, since they didn't leave Poland following the 1831 Rebellion, nevertheless, they were considered as the most influential representatives among the emigrants. Mickiewicz, one of the most important spiritual and patriotic leaders in Polish society, and Chopin, who always identified himself as a Pole in both Polish and French circles, never hesitated to convey their patriotism in their works. Liszt's statement, describing the listener's experiences of Chopin the pianist to be intensified by hearing him perform his own works, may be a good description of these two artists' devotion and the Romantic essences in their art works:

Music was his language, the divine tongue through which he expressed a whole realm of sentiments...As with that other great poet Mickiewicz...the muse of his homeland dictates his songs, and the anguished cries of Poland lend to his art a mysterious, indefinable poetry which, for all those who have truly experienced it, cannot be compared to anything else. (Eisler, p. 86)

CHAPTER IV

METHODOLOGY OF ANALYSIS

The previous chapter illustrates the lives of Chopin and Mickiewicz and their resemblance in background as well as their influences to the Romantic Movement in the nineteenth century. Their mutual friendship was shown not only on the personal level but it also had a profound impact on their professional lives and philosophical thinking. The impact is particularly evident in their artistic works, such as their ballads/ballades. To demonstrate and compare the narrative styles of their ballads and ballades, the following chapter will focus in analyzing the rhythmic structures of Chopin's third ballade associated with the prosody of Mickiewicz's *Świtezianka*.

According to Susanne Langer, the language of music, like poetry, more closely resembles the "morphology of feelings" (*A Guide to Research in Music Education*, p.128). This concept will be a fundamental idea of this study in analyzing the narrative of music by literary reflections. Thus, the author will construct a method to conduct a comparative analysis of both music and literature.

As the expressionists criticize musical analysis, the significance of music encompasses two basic levels, intrinsic and referential. Theorists have concluded that in addition to musical syntax, human emotions and cultural insights importantly symbolized in music must be reported in analysis (*A Guide to Research in Music Education*, pp.124 & 128). As the author concludes in the first chapter, musical elements, including motive, melody, rhythm, phrase, harmony, form, etc., create shapes and styles of narrative to express or to imitate human emotions and vocal expressions. Therefore, besides the intrinsic study, the expressionists believe that music has to be analyzed and interpreted on a deeper emotional and philosophical level.

In this study the author believes that Chopin ballades for piano have a strong connection to Mickiewicz's poetic ballads. According to the biographical relationships and the comparative styles between these two artists, the music of Chopin's ballades encompasses the poetic instincts—the nature of lyricism and drama, and comparatively, Mickiewicz's poetic language is musical in terms of the varied patterns of verbal sounds, rhythms, and phrases.[1] In order to verify the connection between music and words in Chopin's case, the

---

[1] Mickiewicz was highly interested in music since his college years. Rüdiger Ritter, in his presentation held at the 21.6.1998 conference on the occasion of the 200th birthday of Adam Mickiewicz at the University of Bremen, quoted a phrase of Mickiewicz from poet Józef Bohdan Zaleski, which was recorded in Mickiewicz's

author chooses rhythm as a topic to interpret his ballades via the philosophical issues referring to the relationships with Mickiewicz's ballads. The formal analysis is a tool of investigating the intrinsic rhythmic elements in excerpts of both Chopin's ballades and Mickiewicz's ballads. The poetic rhythms in Mickiewicz's ballads, including meters and feet, will be examined, along with conducting a rhythmic analysis of Chopin's ballades based on the dimensional concept of Grosvenor Cooper and Leonard Meyer.

Bruce Finley Taggart, in *Rhythmic Perception and Conception: A Study of Bottom-Up and Top-Down Interaction in Rhythm and Meter*, discusses a direct temporal perception of rhythmic patterns and a conception, or indirect understanding, of large-scale musical segmentation in the study of rhythm. The direct temporal perception of music exists while the music is playing, but during the process of listening the listener is able to organize what he has heard into different levels. For instance, he would recognize the recapitulation because he is able to mentally examine the sounding objects of the exposition with his memory, and makes a conclusion that they are comparatively similar. Therefore, the listener is able to group contiguous notes, motives, and phrases, and as long as the music stretches out in time, his auditory experience would provide him a picture of longer-range musical structures. This ability is also utilized in listening to a speech—the audience perceives syllables, words, and word groups, to form sentences, paragraphs, sections, and the whole story.

Taggart suggests that the perceptual processing is temporally linear, and the listener, either trained or untrained, can experience the lower levels of the music, such as the flow of notes, motives, the steady pulses of the meter, up to phrases. However, outside of the flow of motives and phrases, the next step of higher-level listening involves the relationships of phrases and sections, which becomes a conceptual understanding. Unlike perceptual groupings, which are automatic and subconscious, conceptual structures can be consciously manipulated, and directly lend themselves to verbal description (Taggart, p. 28). As rhythm is patterns of short and long time-spans, the distinction between the perception of rhythmic shapes (short spans) and the conception of rhythmic structures (long spans) is especially significant in the study of rhythm. Durational patterning and subsequent metric format are fundamentally temporal. However, as we look into a higher temporal hierarchy, our perception of durational pattering is reduced. We require stylistic input to establish a higher-

letter out of Lausanne of 7.1.1840, in Adam Mickiewicz, Dzieła XV (= Listy II), Warszawa 1955, letter no. 509, S. 307: "Often I sing, and I would like to write sometime once in addition music; if I have money, understand myself, let lie I both literature and books, would go on the village and would compose music. An old intention is only that however no one believes in my musical talent." (English translation by I-Chen Chen) level rhythmic understanding, and this understanding is not experienced in the same way of perceiving the lower-level fundamental blocks.

Modern theorists, in contrast to Schenkerian theories, such as Cooper and Meyer (1960), Jan LaRue (1970), and Eugene Narmour (1989), follow the intrinsic experiences of the listener, who receives a linear sequence of stresses and releases in a musical composition element-by-element, and constructs a hierarchy from lowest-level groupings to highest-level conceptions as a whole. Unlike the Schenkerian theories, which believe that the abstract and conceptualized high-level structures have control over the rhythmic structure of lower levels, they assume that the feeling of rhythmic structures starts from the fundamental organizing force—the lower-level groupings. The lower-level groupings shape the higher-level rhythmic structures. Under this basic principle, however, their interpretations of small temporal segments are different. Cooper and Meyer describe those segments analogous to poetic feet; LaRue presents the characteristics of rhythmic modules; Narmour, in general, acknowledges the fundamental roles of the rhythmic and metric patterning in his bottom-up musical closure—the "implication-realization" model.

Cooper and Meyer suggest that musical rhythm is formed by patterns of strong and weak accents analogous to those found in poetry. Their methods of rhythmic analysis are strongly practical for this study. The analyses of Cooper and Meyer build up an architectonic structure encompassing three levels in general from lowest to highest: small rhythmic motives, rhythmic groupings, to phrases and periods. In addition, melody, harmony, tone-color, dynamics, texture, and form are taken into account in the analysis of the characteristics of rhythm, such as ambiguity, transformation, mobility, tension, continuity, etc.

The referential study attributes the emotional and cultural qualities and meanings in the intrinsic and formal elements. Emotional qualities and meanings, or as Langer called them, virtual feelings, are interpreted with the corroboration of formal analysis of musical significance. In the case of the rhythmic analysis in Chopin ballades, the rhythmic shapes and structures indeed drive the dramatic momentums in different situations, related to those in Mickiewicz's ballads. In addition, cultural effects engage the onto-historical world of the composer—the life of the composer corresponding to the cultural environment. In this particular study, the personal and artistic influences of the individual poet will be emphasized.

Cooper and Meyer

Cooper and Meyer's book extended Meyer's ideas of musical effect presented in his *Emotion and Meaning in Music* (1956). Their methodology of rhythmic analysis believes that rhythm includes "all the elements which create and shape musical processes" (Cooper and Meyer, p. 1). Cooper and Meyer display the grouping of sounds based on the sequences of stress and release to organize the rhythmic shapes. The sequences of stress and release are the result of the interaction among the varied elements, including pitch, duration, harmony, timbre, and texture. The interaction of temporal groupings with the addition of other shaping forces, such as melody, harmony, counterpoint, and orchestration, provides a higher dimensional observation in the study of rhythm.

Associated with the poetic prosody, Cooper and Meyer organize the musical rhythm in five basic patterns: iamb ($\smile$ $-$)[2], anapest ($\smile$ $\smile$ $-$), trochee ($-$ $\smile$), dactyl ($-$ $\smile$ $\smile$), and amphibrach ($\smile$ $-$ $\smile$). Since a rhythmic organization is architectonic, the rhythmic structures, from smaller rhythmic motives to larger temporal spans—phrases, periods, sections, etc., are exhibited in these basic patterns. Therefore, from bottom to top, these basic patterns establish a temporal hierarchy. Cooper and Meyer write,

Most of the music with which we shall be concerned is architectonic in its organization. That is, just as letters are combined into words, words into sentences, sentences into paragraphs, and son on, so in music individual tones become grouped into motives, motives into phrases, phrases into periods, etc. This is a familiar concept in the analysis of harmonic and melodic structure. It is equally important in the analysis of rhythm and meter. (p. 2)

Cooper and Meyer assert that the metric structure is similarly architectonic (p.2). They present an example of the distinction between the 3/4 and 6/8 meters in that the former is made up of three units of a lower level 2/8 meters, while the latter includes two units of a lower level 3/8 meters. In addition, either one of them can be combined with metric units of the same level to form higher metric levels. In the following example the meter of the primary level in which beats are counted is in threes. The inferior level is formed in two units (2/8) and the higher level is also duple (2 × 3/4) (p. 2):

---

[2] $-$ represents a strong accent, and $\smile$ is a mark for a non-accent.

Ex. 4.1 Opening measures of Presto movement from Schubert's Wanderer-Fantasie

Cooper and Meyer define rhythm as "the way in which one or more unaccented beats are grouped in relation to an accented one" (p. 6); accent is "a stimulus (in a series of stimuli) marked for consciousness in some way" (p. 8). A rhythmic grouping must consist of one accented element and one or more unaccented ones, and each accented element is counted as the focal point whereas the unaccented ones are grouped and in relation to what they are heard. Although rhythm in some ways is influenced by the metric organizations, as the first down beat is usually the accented point in rhythmic sense, nevertheless, sometimes the rhythmic groupings are more difficult to recognize than the metric ones, since rhythmic groupings cross bar lines more often than metric ones.

Rhythm is usually grouped by the influence of other forces, such as unexpected stress, or melodic motion. In example 4.2, the basic unit of the primary level could be the quarter-note, and the strong metric accents fall on every first quarter-note of the measure. However, since the dynamic stresses lie on the third beat, of which the function might be suspected, the stresses become the force to change the metric grouping (Strong Weak Weak) to the amphibrach (WSW). While the stresses are placed on every other quarter-note, and the remaining unaccented ones stay the normal strong-weak pairings of duple meter, the strong-weak pairs can still be seen in Cooper and Meyer's secondary level, which can serve as a rhythmic shaping force. However, when the center of gravity is accounted for by the influence of melodic and harmonic movements, the form of shaping may change in higher levels. As we see in levels three and four, the shape changes to the iamb (weak-strong) pairs.

Ex. 4.2 Minuet from Haydn's London Symphony

The influence of melodic organization upon the rhythmic grouping is emphasized in Cooper and Meyer's theory. They present the opening measures of Chopin's Preludes No. 1 and No. 4 (example 4.3) to illustrate the importance of the melodic influence. The contents of both melodies are similar; both start on the fifth degree of the scale with a non-chord final tone which is one degree higher than the first note. However, in terms of rhythmic grouping, the two preludes are different. Because of the rests separating the melodic groups from one another, the melody of the first prelude doesn't show the end-accented rhythm, which creates a trochaic grouping within each measure. The theorists suggest that the agitated, unstable character of this melody is marked because "a temporal organization which is naturally end-accented has been forced to become beginning-accented" (p. 36). Therefore, a trochaic grouping makes us hear the G moving toward A, instead of the other way around, namely that our aural expectation follows the melodic movements. In the fourth prelude, the rhythmic group follows the melodic natural course—an end-accented iamb grouping. This iamb grouping across the bar lines from C to B creates a descending pattern, which we feel as an expressive, yearning call.

Chopin's prelude No. 1

Chopin's prelude No. 4

Ex. 4.3 The openings of Chopin's preludes No. 1 and No. 4

Cooper and Meyer's rhythmic analyses can be a kind of synthesis containing the issues of melody, harmony, tone-color, and the dynamics. Texture and form are added as other aspects to be considered as well. They believe that a good analysis of one musical factor "describes the effects of all the factors in combination" (p. 117). In fact, the concept of architectonic levels is established by the involvement of other musical aspects; while the listener constructs his rhythmic experience toward higher levels, the realization of longer-span rhythms can be done by the flow of intensity. The flow of intensity is the interaction of musical aspects—melodic shaping, phrasing, harmonic structure, texture, form, etc.

According to the examples which Cooper and Meyer present in their book, we may easily understand how melody and harmony can influence the shaping of rhythmic structure; but how about form? Are we dealing with rhythm when we observe a piece as a sonata-allegro form? In Cooper and Meyer's eyes, form, along with all other musical aspects, provides for continuity of movement (p. 151), and continuity in music is "the sense of connection between any one point of time in a piece and the next point of time" (p. 147). They present Chopin's prelude in E-flat Major to examine the interrelationships among rhythm, continuity, and form. The whole piece keeps the continuity of the triplet figure except in the last three measures. The rhythm on the primary level also presents the continuity of amphibrach groups, since all the groups start on the third beat and end on the second. Furthermore, the highest rhythmic level is also a stretched amphibrach. The A section (measure 1-16) ends on a feminine cadence, while a strong tendency of a dominant in measure 32 to the tonic in the next measure, as well as the interruption of a surprised rest, serves an emphasis of the returning A' (measure 33-49). The contrasting B section (measure 17-32) insures formal continuity by building up a harmonic ambiguity to delay the expected assurance of tonal return. Therefore, the overall rhythmic structure is as below:

Fig. 4.1 The overall rhythmic structure of Chopin E-flat major prelude

Furthermore, the comparison of phrasing among each section, or in Cooper and Meyer's term "morphological lengths", can be amplified through the interconnection of form and rhythm:

A   4+2+2=8
4+2+2=8

B   2+2+4=8

                     2+2+4=8

A'   4+2+2=8

      4+4=8

Coda   2+2+4=8

                    2+2+4=8

                         4(+)

                         2

Fig. 4.2 The phrasing structure of Chopin E-flat major prelude

The rhythms of A and A' are similar, but it is interesting that those of B and the coda are comparably parallel. In terms of harmonic intensity, B is an active passage in tonality, and the upward melodic striving creates a momentum for return. On the other hand, the coda stays close to home tonally, and its melodic function brings the melody always back to the tonic; it ends on an extensional insurance of the tonal return in the last seven measures. Comparing it with B, the coda is "tranquillo" and less articulated.

General speaking, Cooper and Meyer's rhythmic analyses are modeled derived from a listener's temporal experience. Their analyses start from lower levels to higher levels, because all high-level structures are established from the combination and interaction of low-level structures. They observe the rhythmic and metric contradiction and ambiguity in the evaluation of grouping, since they believe both are equally important in a listener's perspective. They suggest that rhythm interacts with other musical factors; all musical factors affect the rhythmic groupings in varied ways.

Langer and Kivy

Referential meaning in music and the arts is a main topic in Susanne Langer's writings. She claims that music, as other arts, is a symbolic system. When we examine symbols in ordinary languages, they are "placed in a context which causes one to refer to other contexts" (Ferrara, p. 7). A single letter "r", for example, does not have any meaning. However, if the letter is combined to other letters "u" and "n" to become a word "run" and put it in a sentence, the word becomes a symbol and its referential meaning is clear. In a symbolic system like language, the syntax, which is grammar, refers to the functional rules governing in a sentence structure; for example, the word "run" is a verb. The referential meaning of the word "run," on the other hand, refers to the action and the idea of the action, which is, to move swiftly on foot. The referential meaning of a word might be varied in different cases, depending on how the user combines it with other words; for example, "run for mayor" or "the engine is running".

According to Langer, music is analogous to language in a way that both consist of syntax and references. Music is rational in some ways while also intuitive, whereas language is marked by discursivity. Music is expressive of man's unique being, and it resembles the logic of the dynamics of human experience. Music presents the metaphorical image of human life; the composer captures the essence of actual life or feeling and transforms it into a virtual form. His evolving knowledge of transforming actual feeling into musical (virtual) feeling reflects the form of emotional conception so that we can understand his music, although we do not experience the music in the same way as the composer did when he composed it.

Therefore, Langer concludes that there are two different modes of symbolic systems: ordinary language, like English, is discursive; non-discursive systems, for example, music, poetry, and the arts, have both rational and intuitive levels. Thus, music is not only required to fulfill the rules of ordinary languages but also to reach out to the world of the non-rational by the philosophical support. She opens up a new approach that musical analysis cannot be only of the rational, discursive like language. She views that music does not actually indicate the meaning of things but expressively articulates the meaning of human feelings.

Peter Kivy is one of the recent writers who concern the function of music as a symbolic system, in which the referential meaning can be examined. In *The Corded Shell*, Peter Kivy investigates the problems of emotive descriptions and seeks a solid method as an alternative guide for musical analysis. He says, "the theme of this study is that, however, expressive qualities are genuine 'objective' qualities of music, and that there are objective criteria for applying expressive terms; further, that there is an intelligible way to understand how this all comes about" (*Sound Sentiment*, p. 60). In his book *Sound Sentiment*, Kivy evaluates different styles of music criticism. First, he refers the writings of Robert Schumann as a biographical type of critique. Schumann, in the article about Ludwig Berger's etudes, talked about the life of the composer rather than the work itself. Second, in an excerpt from Hector Berlioz, he provided a personal account of his feelings about Gluck's music but did not speak directly about the music itself; Kivy would call this type as an autobiographical approach. The third type, which is emotive description, is presented by Donald Tovey's analysis. It finally put the direct description of the music on the table, but Tovey ascribed emotions to the music itself; that is, he described it as if the music "is" sad. For the last type, Kivy gives an example from Grosvenor Cooper and Leonard Meyer's analysis of Haydn's "Surprise" Symphony. Here we only observe the scientific, objective description of the music without any musical references. Kivy believes that this kind of description may not be acceptable by anyone except the musically trained people.

Kivy claims that his theory lies on a distinction between the concepts of "to express" and "is expressive of." He believes that music is not "sad"; therefore, music cannot express sadness, whereas a person is sad so he is able to express sadness. As in Langer's philosophy, Kivy suggests that music is "expressive of" sadness; it provides "sadness" in a virtual, abstract form. He provides a large number of criticisms from the seventeenth and the eighteenth centuries to demonstrate musical expressiveness in different cases. He also points out a "physiological" approach in the fourth chapter of his book to show that music can "arouse" images in one's mind by either imitating the sound or the movement of a real object or by associations with human behaviors. His theory can be summarized by the following statement: "music is expressive in virtue of its resemblance to expressive human utterance and behavior" (*Sound Sentiment*, p. 56).

Kivy views music as expressive of emotion by virtue of its resemblance to expressive utterances and behaviors. Therefore, Kivy names a "contour" model to embellish his theory in explaining the expressiveness of music. Contours are purely musical components, presenting structural resemblances with the features of human behaviors. For example, slow, sad music may portray a structural resemblance with observable slow body movement of expressing sadness, whereas agitated and exciting music may imitate the fast activity of expressing excitement. In addition, his "contour" theory explains that the expressiveness of music, as a function of the habitual association of certain musical features with certain emotive ones, usually bears a structural analogy between music syntax and human expression. Musical syntax, as imitative of the conventions, associated with human expression, and expressive of those conventions, offers objectivity to the study of those conventions. Therefore, when we hear a dissonant appoggiatura or a weeping/sighing figure, we often treat those appoggiaturas of weeping figures as a sign of grief, since they capture the custom of expressing grief or pain. As a music analyst, it is appropriate to consider an appoggiatura or a weeping figure as a conventional usage of grief.

In another book, *Sound and Semblance: Reflections on Musical Representation*, Kivy claims that musical representations have a content related aside of syntax. Music offers representations based on "sound-like" relations, structural analogies, common descriptions, conventional associations, and internal resemblances between notation and things extrinsic to the music itself (Ferrara, p. 21). As in *The Corded Shell*, musical representations need to have connective relationships, which the author always likes to claim as "resemblances," between the music itself and what it represents. Therefore, Kivy identifies his emotive description as a rational foundation for the emotive criticism of music as he concludes *The Corded Shell*,

Music criticism needs not to be "inhuman" to be respectable. For the traditional emotive depictions of music, which the musically "learned" reject as irretrievably subjective, or wholly nonsensical, are really no more defective than our emotive depictions of each other and the world around us, on which, according to the contour model, they are parasitic.....If the argument of this book is correct, and the criteria of musical expressiveness can be identified with those of human expression, the it provides a rational foundation for the emotive criticism of music. (*Sound Sentiment*, p. 149)

CHAPTER V

A RHYTHMIC ANALYSIS OF CHOPIN'S BALLADE OP. 47 AND THE
RELATIONSHIP TO MICKIEWICZ'S ŚWITEZIANKA

The Ballads of Mickiewicz

Style

When Mickiewicz published his first volume of poetry, ballads had already become popular in Polish literature. The Polish ballads by that time, although written by secondary poets, simply used the conventional idiom and followed the traditional form of ballads in other countries. The ballad form had been developed for a long period of time; it is derived from songs preserved and transmitted orally among illiterate or semiliterate people (Albert Friedman, in *Princeton Encyclopedia of Poetry and Poetics*, p. 62). The poems feature single stories with a mixture of dramatic (action and events), lyric (descriptions of nature and scenery), and epic (references of a legendary past, pre-destined world, and the all knowing Narrator) elements (Zakrzewska, 1999). There are three general characteristics in ballads. First, ballads usually concentrate on a single crucial episode or situation, with the events leading to this crucial episode described in a rushed manner. The circumstantial settings are not very important, however, the narrator shows the happenings of a certain period of time. Second, there is always a narrator introducing the story without any subjective attitude toward the event. The voice of ballads is not personal; it could be of a party, a community, or a nation, but never belongs to an individual. Third, the ballad is dramatic. The focus of ballads lies on the intensity and immediacy of the action and the highlighting of emotional impacts in the plot (Albert Friedman, in *Princeton Encyclopedia of Poetry and Poetics*, p.62).

The English had the largest amount of ballads in the world. English ballads in the classical period had the qualities of charm and wit, but later Walter Scott brought back their previous grandeur, as did the Germans. In the ballads of Romantics, the popular ballad narrative was richer in textures borrowed from medieval romances and from minstrel poetry. The main source to track ballads back to medieval and minstrel poetry was folklores. Mickiewicz's introductory essay *On Romantic Poetry* affirmed that folk poetry maintained the spiritual identity with medieval poetry. Folk poetry had preserved the ethos of medieval poetry and its emotional freshness (Weintraub, p. 32).

The native spirit and the supernatural motive, the two main characteristics in folklores, are common topics in Romantic poetry. Romantic poets all over Europe stepped out increasingly to show the vital and mysterious qualities in the human personality in their works, which their ancestors tended to ignore. To express the qualities of the human personality, the stories which the Romantic poets usually chose were from national legends or ancient myths. These stories were spread nationally and their topics were usually love, legendary heroes, historical events, or mythic tragedies, which often contained the national spirit and values or the supernatural power to judge good and evil. As the ballad was influenced by the folk, the language of the ballad was comparably simple and closer to native dialects to keep the tradition of the singing quality in the ballad form.

The style of Mickiewicz's ballads is simple and natural. Neither did Mickiewicz introduce a new literary genre, since the ballad had already been popular in Polish literature, nor did he open the folklore supernatural world, which had been haunting in Polish poems. However, he created a new poetic vocabulary. The poet knew how to use conventional words and phrasing and transform them to a new rhetoric. Czesław Miłosz mentioned that Mickiewicz made use indirectly of popular songs which were often heard in the historical Grand Duchy of Lithuania. He transformed those songs into poems by using the words and phrasings that the Lithuanians were familiar with and retouching them with charm (*Adam Mickiewicz: Poet of Poland*, pp. 60-61).

The topics in his ballads were influenced by European Romanticism. He applied folk beliefs, folk customs, and legends to his poems. In his young age, Mickiewicz admired German authors, especially Schiller, and English ones, especially Scott and Byron. Byronic heroes, like *Konrad Wallenrod*, and mysterious subjects, like *Świtez* and *Świtezianka*, were often utilized in his poems. In addition, the common motive in Romanticism, praise of love and youth, was also employed in his ballads like *Trzech Budrysów*.

Since the common folks were the source of his linguistic inspiration, one of the main elements that Mickiewicz adopted in his ballades is the supernatural. In addition, he explored more seriously the supernatural and its relation to human life. A good example is *Świtez*, a ballade in which Mickiewicz used a popular folk legend. The Świtez is a lake, an actual geographical place in Lithuania. The narrator begins to describe the surroundings of the lake which has been haunted, and later a woman rises out of the waters and tells us how she and her fellow maidens were threatened with death under the attack of Russian invaders. The woman prayed to her gods to save her and her maidens, and finally the water engulfed the city and they became water-lilies. The lake became haunted by their deaths; only the bravest man dares to approach it. As David Welsh states, "Mickiewicz allows us to overhear a narrator who, in turn, sees and overhears what is happening and who persuades us to share his mystification. The dramatic effect is shown by Mickiewicz's usage of the present tense;

everything is happening now, and the narrator is commenting simultaneously (Welsh, p. 24). Furthermore, Mickiewicz presented the real place as a connection to the lives of Lithuanians; the event became a legend of the country.

The ballad *Świtezianka* is also set in this "real" place. Like *Świtez*, the way of storytelling involves the description of visualized scenes and the feelings of characters, from which the clarity and the intensity of the plot emerges to the readers. *Świtezianka* was written in 1821 as the story is about a young hunter who meets a maiden in the wood. She accepts his love with a promise of faithfulness. She then leaves him and he walks homewards beside the lake. He sees another girl at the water's edge, and the fickle lover turns his heart to her and leads her through the marsh. However, the girl is the maiden he met at the first time, the nymph of the lake. She blames him bitterly for his unfaithfulness, drags him down, and drowns him. The spirit of the maiden can be seen dancing in the water, while the ghost of the hunter groans by the old larch tree.

Prosody

Syllabic-accentual meter was used as the norm of prosody by the Polish romantics, such as Mickiewicz, Konopnicka, and Słowacki. The rhythmic patterns are organized by the numbers of syllables and stresses, where all lines of more than eight syllables must have a fixed caesura[1]. Classical poets only admitted feminine rhymes, and the accent lies on the penultimate before the caesura. Romantic poets initiated the masculine rhythms and iambic and anapestic feet in their works. This meter was often used in smaller lyric poems and in sections of dramatic works. Almost all of Mickiewicz' ballads were written in regular syllabic meter with occasional masculine rhythms; in some of them all the lines of the stanza are eight syllables long, in others the second and the fourth lines have eight syllables, and the first and the third are ten or eleven syllables long. However, there are two exceptions, *Trzech Budrysów* and *Zasjeda (The Watch)*, in which the first and the third lines were fourteen syllables, with the caesura in the middle and with internal rhymes, while the second and the fourth lines include ten syllables. Each half of the longer lines is divided into two parts of four and three syllables each; the short lines are divided into three parts: the first of four syllables, and the two following of three syllables each. Thus, each long line has four strong beats, and the shorter ones have three (Weintraub, p. 43).

---

[1] A major pause is made in a line in traditional Polish poetry if the line consists more than eight syllables.

Most of the ballads are in stanzaic form and syllabic prosody, with mostly four line stanzas containing alternating rhymes and rhythms (numbers of syllables per line). A description of the structure of three major ballads is presented as follows:

Title	Number of stanzas	Number of lines per stanza	Number of syllables per line	rhyme
Świteź	48	4	Alternating 11 and 8	abab
Świtezianka	38	4	Alternating 10 and 8	abab
Trzech Budrysów	12	4	Alternating 14 and 10	abcb

Fig. 5.1 The numbers of stanzas, lines, syllables, and rhymes in *Świteź*,
Świtezianka, and *Trzech Budrysów*

The narrative characteristic of ballads has to do with patterning. The patterns in ballad form include two-part, three-part, and symmetrical patterns. David Buchan's study in *The Ballad and the Folk* argues that the purpose of these patterns allowed ballad singers to create new versions of their songs at each performance (p. 87-88). James Parakilas suggests that poets imitating folk-ballads in the eighteenth and nineteenth centuries followed the usage of patterns not because they needed them as folk-ballad singers did, but because the patterns "would help give their poems a tone reminiscent of medieval minstrelsy in general and of ballads in particular" (Parakilas, p. 46).

All those patterns can be found in various levels—from lines and stanzas, to scenes and groups of scenes. Ballads usually present contrasts with balances, antitheses, appositions, and parallelisms in two-part structure, and make repetitions in three-part structure (Parakilas, pp. 46-47). The repetitions are seldom the same, but more often they are repetitions with variation each time. The three-part structure of repetition can also be seen in Chopin's ballades (i.e. the fourth ballade is divided in three main sections by the variations of the main theme). Finally, there are symmetrical structures in ballads. For example, in Mickiewcz' *Świtezianka* the poet framed the poem with similar stanzas at the beginning and the end.

To sum up, the alternation of rhyme and rhythm, repetition, and variation in ballad form have strong musical connotations, and ballade composers highlight these narrative features with "analogous musical techniques" (Parakilas, p. 47).

The Ballades of Chopin

Form

It is well-recognized that Chopin's musical style took a new direction following his departure from Poland in 1830. Indeed at this time Chopin faced serious factors that caused his growth to maturity in his music: a fundamental change in Chopin's self-worth as Warsaw's admiration became Vienna's indifference; a rising disappointment with the career of a concert pianist; a strong commitment to his native country for its uprising of 1830. The result was a big change in Chopin's personal life as well as his approach to composition.

The stylistic transformations were essential in Chopin's new-found forms in the 1830's. The works written in his Warsaw's years such as rondos, variations, and early nocturnes were in the brilliant manner and modeled closely to classical archetypes. Controlled in the classical approach of forms, Chopin created extraordinary contrapuntal textures, ornamental melodies, and a long-range harmonic vision. Following the developments of texture, melody and harmony in the early 1830's, Chopin took on new dimensions of organic designs and tonal structures of German tradition—ballades, scherzos, and fantasies (Samson, in *The Cambridge Companion to Chopin*, p. 102). All three genres have their own demands on form and structure, but they can be referred to a large-scale ternary or sonata-based[2] design. The scherzos maintain the figuration and melody of brilliant style in a simple ternary design, where the divisions are clear and sections are contrasted. The two fantasies (Op. 49 and Op. 61 Polonaise-fantaisie) share a multi-sectional structure, a wide-range of contrasting materials and the characteristic gestures of improvisation; both fantasies have a "slow movement" at the center which have identical tonality—B major. The ballades, however, are presented in a "through-composed, directional structure, where variation and transformation are seminal functions, integration and synthesis essential goals" (Samson, in *The Cambridge Companion to Chopin*, p. 112).

Jim Samson suggests that Chopin's four ballades are of sonata form based on the interaction of two contrasting themes. Carl Dahlhaus also writes that the first ballade "distantly recalls sonata form, being based on an underlying contrast of themes"; "this is fully in the spirit of the 'contrasting derivation' principle found in Beethoven's sonata forms." (Dahlhaus, p. 148). Beyond the regular sonata form, both the first and the fourth ballades have introductions which lead into the first theme of the exposition. The introduction of the first ballade has the characteristic of being recitative, a perfect merge toward the first theme's

---

[2] Jim Samson suggests that all Chopin's ballades are designed by a sonata-based form. See *Chopin: The Four Ballades*, pp. 45-68.

"aria." On the other hand, the introduction of the F minor one initiates motivically with the first theme—the repeated-note pattern, which later returns unexpectedly before the recapitulation.

Yet it cannot be simply said his ballades are of sonata form. Unlike the clear divisions by thematic contrasts and harmonic events in the normal sonata form, the structure of Chopin's ballades reveals a synthesis of the three-part architecture and the variations of emotional contexts associated with literary influences. John Rink takes a detailed study of the first ballade by Serge Gut (1989) to demonstrate how Chopin explored the formal principles from the literary ballad in his piano music. Gut's study suggests that the work is structured according to "musical content" and "tonality and style (lyric, dramatic, epic, and virtuosic, etc.)," and shows the relationships between differences in styles (language) and themes and tonalities (structure):

Section	Introduction	I A	(86 bars)		II A'	(32 bars)
Subsection		1	2	3	4	5
Bars	1-7	8-35	36-67	68-93	94-105	106-125
Number of bars	7	28	32	26	12	20
Musical content	Figuration	Theme I	Bridge	Theme II	Theme I	Theme II
Tonality	g	g	g	E-flat	a	A
Style	Narrative	Narrative	Narrative/lyric	Lyric	Narrative/epic	Lyric/epic

Section	III B	(40 bars)		IV A''	(42 bars)	Coda
Subsection	6	7	8	9	10	11
Bars	126-137	138-149	150-165	166-193	194-207	208-264
Number of bars	12	12	16	28	14	57
Musical content		Pianistic figurations		Theme II	Theme I	Figuration
Tonality	E-flat	E-flat	E-flat	E-flat	g	g
Style		Dramatic virtuosity		Lyric	Narrative/epic	Dramatic

Fig. 5.2 Formal structure of Chopin G minor Ballade by Serge Gut (Rink, p. 109)

As shown above, there are three completely independent structural components: the dramatic first theme, the lyrical second theme, and improvisational sections—all pianistic and virtuosic figurations. It is clear that the ballade is neither of regular sonata form, nor of the balanced ternary form—an A' section interrupts between A and B sections by a rare tonal interaction (A parallel major and minor). The ballade deals with conflicts of melodic ideas, as similar as literary ballads which often include characters' personalities in conflict with each other; those melodic ideas, however, are not presented in their original form twice. Earlier composers, in their sonata-allegro forms, tended to stabilize their themes in the recapitulation and led them into the tonic key. Chopin's themes are subject to the aesthetic purpose, yet they often become an aggrandizement, not a return in their original form. Furthermore, the returning themes purposely leave something incomplete and conclude with decorated materials and musical expansions. The final moments always increase power and tempo, imitating the common dramatic finale of the folk ballads as described in Friedman's description of the folk ballad: "at last the final and revelatory substitution bursts the pattern, achieving a climax and with it a release of powerful tensions" (Albert Friedman, in *Encyclopedia Britannica: Macropedia*, volume 23, p. 107).

The other common feature in the four ballades is that Chopin juxtaposes the two contrasting themes and that they "reach their new altered form, an apotheosis" (Neil Witten, p. 386). The interaction of both themes is not temporary but an "irreversible metamorphosis, demonstrating organic and musical growth" (Neil Witten, p. 387). In earlier sonata form, the theme-groups merge and interact with each other in the development sections, but they are often separated and presented in their original form; the thematic fragments may develop and repeat in order to construct a passage of transition or an entire development section, but they often retain a similar personality and shape as in the exposition. However, in the development sections of Chopin's ballades, the combination of two themes becomes a process of growth in texture and tension. Chopin uses fragments from the two themes from the previous sections but, instead of repeating from the original shapes, transforms them into a new gesture. Here is a reminder of the thematic relationships in each ballade:

G minor Ballade:

F Major Ballade:

Theme A:

Theme B:

A + B

85

A-flat Major Ballade:

Theme A:

Theme B:

A + B

F minor Ballade:

Ex. 5.1 Thematic relationships in four ballades

Inspired by a single-lined succession of actions in folk ballads, the ballades possess an organic unity so that Chopin seems to "follow a story" (Newcomb, 1987). This organic unity is formed by the significant thematic transformation and rhythmic similarity. Thus, the uniqueness of the ballades lies on the special development of successions of themes, which marks the structural logic that concretizes the ballades. Leichtentrill observes that the structure of Chopin's ballades combines the elements of the lied (variations of texture, sonority, and periodic phrasing inspired by the stanzaic form), rondo (the repetition of motivic and rhythmic fragments), sonata (two contrasting themes in each ballade), and variation set (variations in themes) (Rink, p. 101). And Jim Samson assumes that,

In the Chopin ballades transformation processes are cumulative, concerned with the gradual enrichment of a theme through variation, textural expansion and contrapuntal intensification. Material seldom returns in its original state, though the process of variation may affect only minor details. (*Chopin: The Four Ballades*, p. 78)

Therefore, this characteristic becomes a cyclic link among the four ballades. In Jim Samson's study of Chopin's ballades the focus on revealing the analogy of melodic and rhythmic contour of themes addresses the "unity of form and expression":

First Ballade

Ex. 5.2 The melodic and rhythmic contour of themes in four ballades
(*Chopin: The Four Ballades*, p. 73)

Samson observes that the themes of the four ballades share the same rhythmic features and the falling-motion motive, and he believes that this cross-reference is a basic character of their thematic materials such that "the ballades are most obviously part of a single genre" (*Chopin: The Four Ballades*, p. 73).

There is another gesture, mentioned by Neil Witten, that the melodic ending 2-3-1, an emphasis on the penultimate third degree of the scale, is regarded as a "potentially characteristic ballade device" (pp. 172-173):

G minor Ballade:

F Major Ballade:

A-flat Major Ballade:

Ex. 5.3 The 2-3-1 gesture in themes of three ballades

In addition, the initial "upbeats" in theme I of G minor, theme I of F Major, theme II of A-flat Major, and theme I and II of the F minor seem to be a cross-reference to this single genre. To conclude, cyclic links of a thematic kind interlock all four ballades and establish a specific genre that was never used before for instrumental music.

Rhythm

"The emphasis is on a single line of action precipitously developed," writes Albert Friedman about ballads (*Princeton Encyclopedia of Poetry and Poetics*, p. 62). It is significant that Chopin narrated a story in a single, uninterrupted work, since many narrative instrumental works before Chopin had been episodic in form. Johann Kuhnau's six biblical sonatas published in 1700, titled such as *Saul's Madness Cured by Music, The Conbat between David and Goliath*, etc., represent stories from the Old Testament told in music; they consist of many small independent episodes to describe different scenes of the story. Vivaldi's *The Four Seasons* adapts a traditional sequence of movements for the stories. Furthermore, even a narrative program tends to be illustrated in a traditional multi-movement form, such as Beethoven's *Pastoral Symphony*.

Chopin's ballades are remarkable among the narrative instrumental works of his time, for the reason that Chopin was loyal to the "single line of action, precipitously developed" of the folk ballad model. Each of his ballades unfolds a unified musical form, and within that form each of them develops "a powerful rhythmic momentum of a sort that is almost unprecedented in earlier music" (Parakilas, p. 52). The momentum, that each of the ballades carries forward by its own, leads to a climax at the end through the sequences of, as Parakilas says, "leaping and lingering"—some sections increase speed and others hold back (p. 52). The most striking changes are in the first and second ballades; Chopin changes tempo, meter, and material at the end of the short introduction and before the coda in the first ballade, and he uses the contrasting tempo and character of two alternating main themes in the second ballade:

First Ballade:

Introduction

Second Ballade:

First theme

Second theme

Ex. 5.4 The changes of tempo and meter in the first and second ballades

The third and the fourth ballades have less internal contrasts of tempo, but they gradually build up the momentum by the flow of notes, phrases, and sections from the beginning to the end.

Although they utilize different combinations of "leaping" and "lingering", all four ballades are built in an uninterrupted span of music toward the climax at the end. The effect of continuous variations in a single increase of momentum is drawn from the folk ballad in which a story unfolds from a mysterious opening, then a chaotic development, to the final reckoning—as in the case of music Chopin puts a coda or a finale in each of his ballades. Each of the ballades starts in a slow-side and steady tempo, but the final moment always reaches the climax by a faster and restless pace. The increasing energy from the beginning to the end is a distinguishing feature of Chopin's ballades; however even more obviously the common metric feature in all four ballades is another rhythmic characteristic that makes them more distinctive than other narrative works.

All four ballades have a common metric feature—6/4 or 6/8. According to Jim Samson's comment, 6/8 or 6/4 was a frequently used meter for music which was associated with narrative and pastoral qualities in the eighteenth and early nineteenth centuries. It is significant that ballad settings by Schubert, Loewe and others were often presented in this type of meter (Samson, *Chopin: The Four Ballades*, p. 11). The sextuple rhythm, mostly used in nocturnes and barcarolles, gives not only a dreamlike and lyrical quality but also a rolling movement which easily unfolds the story from beginning to end. It especially brings out the motions of poetic feet in ballad verses, which gives this new genre its own characteristic of rhythm.

Chopin Ballade Op. 47 and *Świtezianka*

According to Schumann's reviews, Chopin indeed mentioned particular ballads of Mickiewicz which inspired his own ballades; but since Schumann didn't record the names of Mickiewicz's ballads from which Chopin received inspiration, today we don't know which particular ones Chopin's ballades were based on. However, many scholars agree that the tonal and harmonic systems Chopin created in his ballades establish a narrative style of his own. They suggest that an intimate relationship between the ballades of Chopin and the ballads of Mickiewicz exists (Samson, Keefer, and Zakrzewska), and possible particular ballads of Mickiewicz have been assigned to Chopin's four ballades. This tradition refers the first ballade to link with Mickiewicz's *Konrad Wallenrod*, the third ballade with *Świtezianka*, and the fourth ballade with *Trzech Budrysów*; *Świtez and Świtezianka* have both been assigned to the second ballade at different times. Such links with Mickiewicz's ballads were a common thought of the nineteenth century music criticism, and it encouraged a perspective of wordless narrative toward these works. Therefore, the following rhythmic analysis presents the third ballade and *Świtezianka* as a representative of the narrative relationship between Chopin's ballades and Mickiewicz's ballads.

The rhythmic structure of *Świtezianka* is organized in couplet form (four lines in each stanza, two pairs of stresses in the first and the third lines) with subdivision of tripodies (dactyl, trochee, amphibrach). The mixture of duple and triple rhythms is also the common character in the four ballades of Chopin; they are all set in a similar sextuple metrical structure—6/4 in the first one (except the introduction), and 6/8 in the others. Each measure is made of two large beats triply subdivided. Although sextuple meter is common in folk-ballad and ballad Lieder, nevertheless, Chopin brings out a similar rhythmic character in all four ballades. Parakilas states,

At or near the beginning of each ballade, that rhythm is heard at a moderate speed and with a quiet lilt, giving the music the character—stronger at some times than at others—of a nocturne or a barcarolle (p. 54).

In each of the ballades there are accompaniments in the arpeggiated rhythms typical of

Chopin's nocturnes, and melodies in the barcarolle rhythm, a mixture of  and

. The rhythm brings to the ballades the poetic associations of nocturne
and barcarolle: night, dream, love, and song. In other words, it gives Chopin's ballades the
same nocturnal settings as the Romantic poets gave to their poetic ballads, with the same
implications of a dreamlike quality in the stories of ballads (Parakilas, p. 55).

The total number of stanzas in *Świtezianka* is 38, with four lines in each stanza. The
rhymes are alternated in the form of "abab"—the first and the third lines have the same
rhyme, as the second and the fourth lines share another rhyme. The first lines of each stanza
have 10 syllables with 4 stresses, divided in 5 + 5; the second lines are 8 syllables with 3
stresses. The following presents the numbers of syllables and the locations of the stresses in
the first two stanzas:

texts	numbers of syllables	meter

Jakiż to/ chłopiec// piękny i/ młody?   10 (5+5)

(Dactyl/   Trochee//   Dactyl/   Trochee)

Jaka to/ obok/ dziewica?   8

(Dactyl/   Trochee/   Amphibrach)

Brzegami/ sinej// Świteziu/ wody   10

(Amphibrach/   Trochee//   Amphibrach/   Trochee)

Idą/ przy świetle/ księżyca.   8

(Trochee/   Amphibrach/   Amphibrach)

93

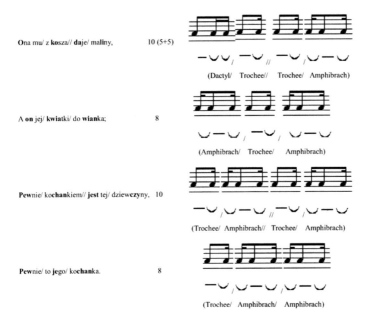

Ona mu/ z kosza// daje/ maliny,   10 (5+5)

(Dactyl/ Trochee// Trochee/ Amphibrach)

A on jej/ kwiatki/ do wianka;   8

(Amphibrach/ Trochee/ Amphibrach)

Pewnie/ kochankiem// jest tej/ dziewczyny,   10

(Trochee/ Amphibrach// Trochee/ Amphibrach)

Pewnie/ to jego/ kochanka.   8

(Trochee/ Amphibrach/ Amphibrach)

Fig. 5.3[3] The numbers of syllables and the locations of the stresses in the first two stanzas in *Świtezianka*

The dactyl, consisting of a stressed syllable followed by two unstressed ones, is used often in classical poetry, especially in hexameter poems. Mickiewicz makes a bold experience on hexameter in the song "The Tale of Wajdelota" in his *Konrad Wallenrod*. The "Tale" consists six feet and six stresses placed regularly in each line, and each of the lines has different numbers of syllables, ranging from thirteen to seventeen. Each foot starts with one strong beat followed by one or two weak syllables; most of the feet are dactyls. In addition, he introduces one feature of the traditional Polish meter, a fixed caesura: a word division after the third foot. This is called Polish hexameter.

The story of the ballad combines two motives from folklore: that of a young hunter being loved by a water nymph, and that of the punishment of an unfaithful lover by eternal damnation. These two motives symbolize "falling"—i.e. the nymph is falling in love and falling into a struggling situation of unfaithfulness, and later she drags the young man down

---

[3] The author inserts the musical imitation of poetic feet by writing them as pure musical rhythms above.

94

to the lake. Mickiewicz was inspired by Polish folks and duma[4] of terror and made brilliant use of mysterious, supernatural, and tragic elements in his ballads. In this ballad, Mickiewicz uses many trochaic feet, the rhythm which has a stressed syllable followed by an unstressed one. The rhythm of the trochaic foot imitates the motion of "falling" (Parker, in *Princeton Encyclopedia of Poetry and Poetics*, p. 870), and is often interpreted as abrupt and impulsive (Sorantin, p. 36).[5] Chopin uses it to create an atmosphere of "dragging" or "falling" toward the tragic ending. The human, revealing guilt, actually falls into the control of devil, the higher judgment and punishment over human beings. The falling motion tells of a mysterious sadness.

In Chopin's ballade op. 47, the feature of the main motive displays a motion of falling with a trochaic rhythmic shape:

Ex. 5.5 The trochaic shape of the motive of the third ballade

This main motive creates an issue of shifting metrical accent. Theoretically, F, the third eighth note of measure 2, is considered a weak up-beat; from the standard of Cooper and Meyer's book *The Rhythmic Structure of Music*, F as a weak beat following E-flat as the down beat seems to be profiled as an iambic figure. However due to the descending melodic shape F—E-flat and the harmonic resolution, from the diminished 7th chord with the bottom of dominant E flat to the second inversion of the tonic chord, an agogic stress is located on the upbeat, the eighth-note F. Additionally the slur on the left-hand chords supports the stress on the diminished 7th and the release on the second inversion of the tonic chord. Therefore, the motive shapes a trochaic contour.

Harmonically the first measure is basically under the dominant E-flat seventh chord, followed by a second-inversion tonic harmony in the second measure. The following two

___

[4] Dumy (pl. duma), a type of Ukrainian oral poetry. They appear to date from the 16th and later centuries and deal with leaders and nameless heroes who suffered in tragic situations and wars. See *Princeton Encyclopedia of Poetry and Poetics*, p. 876.
[5] See more musical examples in *The Problem of Musical Expression* by Erich Sorantin, pp. 36-57.

measures maintain the same harmonic progression. Thus, the harmonic stress tends to lie on the second and the forth measures, which is "dominant resolving to tonic" iambic motion. However, the entire first theme is trochaic. The opening E-flat, the dominant note, slides up by a diatonic scale in two directions: the right hand up to the C with the left hand down to the tonic A-flat. From the first note of the piece to the first note of the second measure, the harmony changes in every single note. The harmonic rhythm of the first two measures is speedy, but it slows down in measures 3 and 4. Therefore, the rhythmic flow is basically a trochaic "fast (harmonic tension)—slow (release)" motion (Ex. 5.6). The second part of the first theme follows the same pattern (Ex. 5.7). Later on, the F—E-flat motive appears as the controlling motive idea through measures 9 to 12. Within a simple harmonic rhythm of I—V, the left hand continues the idea of F—E-flat motive with the pick-ups of the thread E-flat octaves played by the right hand (Ex. 5.8). In measures 13 to 16 the game continues. The left-hand parallel sixths have the rapid dotted rhythm borrowed from the right hand in measure 10; the whole phrase is an agitated echo of the previous one.

Chopin uses the descending F—E-flat motive as the vehicle to organize the melodic and rhythmic shapes beginning in measure 9. The opening phrase highlighted by two-note descents (F—E-flat, D-flat—C) make a trochaic rhythmic shape (Ex. 5.9 and 5.10).

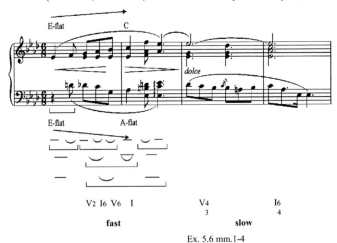

Ex. 5.6 mm.1-4

harmonic rhythm: **fast**   **slow**

Ex. 5.7 mm.5-8, the second part of the first theme follows the same pattern as above

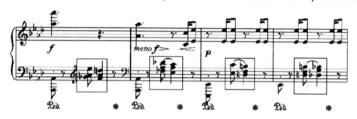

Ex. 5.8 mm.9-12

Ex. 5.9 mm.1-4

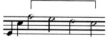

L.H.

Ex. 5.10 The outline of the highlighted notes in the first theme

The descending two-note motive continues in the left hand from measures 9-16 with the melodic expansion:

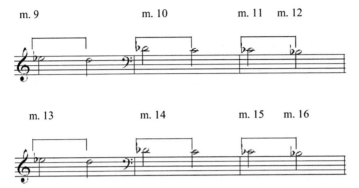

Ex. 5.11 The descending two-note motive in the left hand in mm. 9-16

Later, the right hand takes over in measures 17 through 24.

In measure 25, the octave G-flats give a hint into a new section. The trills in
measures 26 and 28 stay firmly as the focus of the entire measure, and the intensity releases
through the following arpeggios, flying in opposite directions in both hands. The G-flats in
measure 25 are ambiguous, and the intensity of G-flats extends to the trill of the next measure,
but eventually was resolved to F dominant arpeggios and B-flat octaves. This pattern shows
up again with an additional B-natural in the left hand to create a smooth chromatic bass line.
Later on the pattern condenses and repeats for four times.

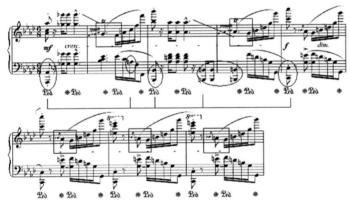

Ex. 5.12 mm.25-32

Next, the passage of the C major transition toward the recapitulation of the first theme begins
a modal of rhythmic conflicts. In the right hand, the rhythmic activity contracts the steady
harmonic rhythm. The melodic shape of the sixteenth notes makes four groups of three-note
cells per measure to contradict the well-established six metrical beats:

Ex. 5.13 The three-note cells in mm. 33-35

The descending shape of the three-note cells echo the motive of F—E-flat, which is a sign of the trochee, and was amplified in the left hand as well:

Ex. 5.14 mm.33-35

This specific rhythmic conflict—the so called hemiole—is not the first encounter we have; its similar rhythmic intensity appears in the other three ballades as well. In the first ballade, starting from measure 48, the right hand eighth-note figure forms four three-note groups in each measure emphasized by perfect and augmented 4th, while the left hand maintains the steady six metrical beats:

Ex. 5.15 mm.48-55, the first ballade

In the second ballade, the hemiole forms differently. In measure 47, the sixteenth-note figure of the right hand sets in three four-note groups, and the left hand stays on two groups of eighth-notes figure. The 47th measure, considered as larger three against two hemeola, reverses its combination in the next measure: three-note groups in the left hand against two-note ones in the right hand.

Ex. 5.16 mm.47-48, the second ballade

In the fourth ballade, Chopin uses the hemiole in the third-time recapitulation of the first theme section as a contrast with the beginning and the second-time variation. The right hand melody becomes more chromatic and improvisatorial, starting at measure 152, while the left hand keeps the steady three-notes grouping. Later, the right hand, from measure 157, begins to have sixteenth-note triplets and makes a rhythmic three (right) against two (left) hemiole between both hands. This intense rhythmic texture is used again in the coda between measures 227 to 230.

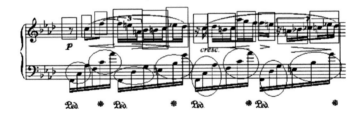

Ex. 5.17 mm.152-153, the forth ballade

Ex. 5.18 mm.157-158, the forth ballade

Within the framework of metrical convention for a four-measure period, Chopin uses irregular rhythmic activity to establish an intense or uncertain atmosphere either for transition passages or for a contrasting repetition with the previous ones. The rhythmic irregularity in measures 33-35 in this particular third ballade displays a vague and disoriented manner, while the C major, with sonority dominating this passage, seems to predictably modulate into F, but only after the isolated C octave glides up chromatically to E-flat in the left hand; the restatement of the first theme comes back surprisingly in A-flat major.

Beginning measure 37, the first theme comes back; however, after four measures, the sequential fragments from the first theme develop. The left hand shows the ascending six-note scale-fragment, contrasting with the right hand's trochee motive on the top voice sequentially:

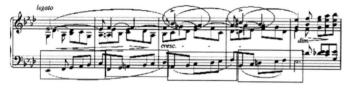

Ex. 5.19 mm.41-49

The F—E-flat motive is already an important contour, and the climax built up by the sequential fragments arrives at measures 45 and 46, where the opening phrase was stated. Echoing the F—E-flat motive in a higher octave, Chopin breaks the routine of a four-measure period and expands it to five measures. Neil Witten suggests,

Had Chopin not inserted the extra measure, the end of the phrase (m. 49) would have coincided with the end of several four-measure groups, and the metric accent of the next group would have fallen on the A-flat chord in measure 50. Instead, the displacement renders the metric accent on C on the down-beat of measure 49. (p.183)

In other words, the five-measure phrase is for the purpose of highlighting C, which is extended to the next second-theme section:

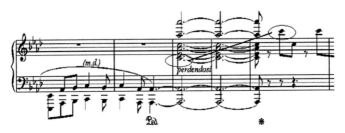

Ex. 5.20 mm.48-52

Additionally, the whole first-theme section ends on the A-flat chord with the bass C. It seems that Chopin tried to make a smooth transition to the broken C octaves in the beginning of the second theme section.

Chopin emphasizes the gravity of the trochaic rhythm through descending intervals and large leaps; especially in the second-theme section, the broken C octave motive, starting in measure 51, increases the intensity of the falling motion.

Ex. 5.21 The falling motion of the second theme

Rhythmically the second theme controls the complexity, something that is rarely seen in Chopin's works. Beginning from measure 54, the left hand starts its four-bar group on the first beat of measure 54, while the right hand starts its period two beats later. Chopin puts the melodic notes and supporting chords on unaccented eighth-notes, and the chords always resolve to a single note located on the following accent beat; later in measure 65 the left hand begins a new group, while the right hand delays almost a full bar until the upbeat of measure 66. The displacements of the initial melodic notes create a different nuance in performance. Furthermore, Chopin puts slurs on each of the two eights to enforce the unaccented eights. Therefore, as in the F—E-flat motive in the first theme, the broken C octave figure seems to be an iambic motion but is performed as a trochaic motion:

Ex. 5.22 mm.54-58

The proper performance for this passage is simple and graceful, but the dislocated rhythmic emphasis rises performance problems. The metric shift in the musical texture creates the puzzling uncertainty, which however is eased by Chopin's plain pedaling; the result becomes as Alan Rawsthorne described "a charming lurching effect" (qtd. in Neil Witten, p.186).

Although the displacement of the rhythm dominates the second theme section, the melodic structure firmly maintains the basic four-measure period:

Ex. 5.23 The four-measure period of the second theme

Once again, Chopin creates the rhythmic complexity within a firm and square framework of the four-measure period. We can say that Chopin's music has freedom and fantasy but in a structure that has been established since the classical era.

After two four-measure phrases, the last one ends on C major with a surprising A-flat in the left hand; the D-natural and E-natural in the following two measures are a hint of future tonality. Finally the F-minor section comes in with power and confidence. The right hand keeps the trochaic rhythmic style as before, a syncopated accented weak beat followed by a soft down beat, while the rest of the melody contains the dotted rhythmic motive which derives from the development episode in the first theme section. However, the left hand shows a strong iambic rhythm—an upper-register chord keeps the intensity toward a lower strong bass. Therefore, this is a section that performs two contrasting rhythmic feelings simultaneously.

The phrase from measure 65 is built on an unbalanced phrasal period; while the F minor is set firmly in the first two measures, Chopin slides back to A-flat major by using a chromatic bass line F—F-flat—E-flat (fifth of A-flat) in measure 67 and extends the phrase to an unusual 4½ measures. Later the F minor comes back, but the harmonies modulate more quickly to the dominant C; therefore, the phrase is squeezed into three measures. The left hand keeps the iambic figure only for one measure; in the following measure, although the slurs still show the spirit of the figure, the eighth-rests of the figure are filled up with upper-neighbor and passing notes. Chopin even puts staccatos on those eighths to show their softness:

Ex. 5.24 mm.71-72

From measure 73, the sonority remains on the dominant over a C pedal, as the descending melodic line in the soprano is accentuated owing to a doubled line in the left hand. In measure 73 and 74 the melody is spiritually softer due to the quarter rests among the melodic chords; however, the following repetition becomes stronger with longer values of the chords. The final destination arrives on an authoritative F minor, and the left hand begins to have a rhythm parallel with the melody.

In measure 88-94, the fragment coming from the second theme repeats frequently:

m.55   m.88

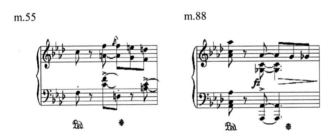

mm.90-94

Ex. 5.25 mm.90-94

The first two fragments in measures 88 and 90 share the same harmonic progression: dominant to tonic in D-flat. However, the following ones have varied modulations. Measure 92 has a G half-diminished seventh chord followed by a C major triad; the second cadence is built from a G dominant seventh. All the cadences are preparing for the coming dominant C to F minor.

After the focused rhythmic displacement of the second theme section, between measures 95 and 102, the game stops temporarily and sets up a simple iambic gesture:

Ex. 5.26 mm.95-99.

Then a section of speedy harmonic rhythms with two beautiful cadences follows, and finally ends on the C major triad to connect the return of the second theme:

Ex. 5.27 mm.100-103.

This return ends on an ambiguous C major for another three measures to initiate a new section:

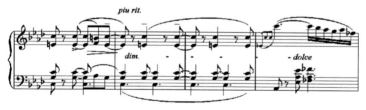

Ex. 5.28 mm.113-116.

The insistence of the rhythmic displacement, as Jim Samson indicates, is "in the sharpest possible contrast to the ensuing waltz episode" (*The Cambridge Companion to Chopin*, p. 118). This new section, a charming waltz, offers a relief from the ambiguity of the second theme section with lots of improvisatory running figures in the right hand. The melodic shape in the right hand maintains the trochaic structure as in the opening theme:

mm. 1-2

mm. 116-117

Ex. 5.29 The melodic shapes of mm. 1-2 and mm. 116-117

In addition, the left hand provides a metric support with the famous iamb figures:

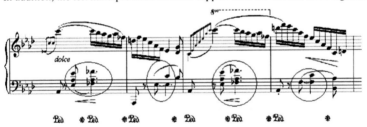

Ex. 5.30 mm.116-119

The iambic rhythm is indeed a special characteristic of all four ballades that it can be well

regarded as a genre marker (Samson, *The Cambridge Companion to Chopin*, p. 118):

Ex. 5.31 mm.65-69, first ballade

Ex. 5.32 mm.1-6, second ballade

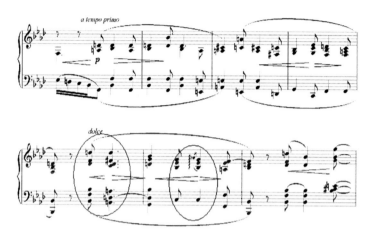

Ex. 5.33 mm.79-85, forth ballade

The iambic rhythm is not only a sign of the ballade form, but is also a major rhythmic characteristic of the barcarolle:

Ex. 5.34 mm. 39-40, Chopin Barcarolle op. 60

The iambic rhythm, the reverse of the trochaic, is the imitation of "rising" motion. Its rising motion implies the characteristic of human movements; Erich Sorantin believes that the emphasis of the iambic and anapestic rhythm, in general or in certain specific patterns, corresponds mainly to human motor activity and symbolizes either pendular or circular movement (p. 74). Therefore, the iambic rhythm in specific 6/8 or 6/4 meters contains the manner of "flowing narrative" (Samson, *Chopin: The Four Ballades*, p. 73). In addition, the general shape of all four ballades tends to be end-weighted, which is a similar manner of "iamb"; the earlier stages are maintained in a low temperature and tension gradually is built toward the end. The end-weighted structure actually comes from the narrative flow of Mickiewicz's poetic ballads, in which the climax is usually saved till the end. In Chopin's ballades, the blaze always fires up at the final moments, except for a contrastingly quiet conclusion that follows the agitated coda in the second ballade.

The iambic figure later transforms into a strong waltz-like rhythm presented by the left hand in this light and sweet episode. The down beats, supposedly the strong beats, are shorter and softer than the weak beats—longer and emphasized by using full chords or trills (the fourth ballade). The trochaic waltz rhythm actually performs an iambic motion. The first and forth ballades also include waltzes in similar manners:

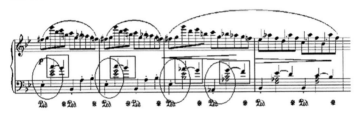

Ex. 5.35 mm.138-141, first ballade

Ex. 5.36 mm.112-114, forth ballade

Ex. 5.37 mm.124-127, third ballade

The phrase structure in this section, between measures 124-135, seems to be odd. The beginning is a four-measure phrase in A-flat major, which becomes a dominant and resolves to D-flat. The first two measures of the D-flat major phrase are a repetition of the previous one; but, starting with measure 130, the D-flat major phrase keeps its expansion by a long improvisatory melodic arc for four measures, with the left-hand rhythmic motives borrowed from previous sections. The last two measures, 134 and 135, is a transition via trills with a

B-flat minor sonority, a ii7 in A-flat major leading to the A-flat finally in measure 144. In addition, the D-flat phrase expands its length from measure 130 by a scale hanging on a single pitch of F, which later is resolved to E-flat in measure 136. Among these measures, the harmonic progression begins on D-flat, followed by a passing B-flat minor, and goes up to an E-flat dominant chord, which will be resolved to an A-flat in measure 144.

The following section is a transition in preparation for the final destination, a return of the second theme. The right hand plays the variants of F—E-flat motive and descending-scale figures continuously:

Ex. 5.38 The variants of F—E-flat motive in mm. 136-142

The left hand keeps the sixteenth-note broken chords to support the triumph moment here; in measure 140 the left hand rolls up to high A-flat while the right hand goes an octave higher with a syncopated eight note beforehand, making the left hand arpeggio observable.

The return of the second theme is in D-flat major, derived from the A-flat dominant octaves during measures 144 and 145. The rhythm keeps the same one as in previous appearances, and the F-flat in measures 149, 153 to 156 prepare for the parallel D-flat minor in measure 157 (enharmonically written in C-sharp minor). The melody from measure 157 is a literary repetition of the melody in the F-minor section:

mm.65-69

mm.157-161

Ex. 5.39 The return of F-minor theme (mm. 65-69) in mm. 157-161

However, the gesture of the melody has changed. Rhythmically, the F-minor section contains rests and dotted rhythms, while the C-sharp minor version portrays legato-staccato contrasts but even eighth-notes. The rests and dotted rhythms in the previous F-minor section echo the rhythm of the left hand figure; as a matter of fact, the legato-staccato eighth notes aid in the generation of momentum from the running figure of the left hand, following the syncopated accents which create the effect of metric dislocation. With the melodic turns and chromatic fragments borrowing from the basic F—E-flat motive, the left-hand accompaniment holds the energy of this section incredibly. The falling second motives, which are mostly located on the weak beats, strengthen the iambic effect of metric displacement:

Ex. 5.40 The falling second motives in the left hand in mm. 157-160

The left hand, from measure 165, takes over the syncopated feature of melody, while the right hand simultaneously keeps up the G-sharp pedal tone spreading over three registers. The syncopation continues, but the descending melodic line expands to a fifth, not a fourth as in the right hand of measures 157 and 158:

mm.157-158

mm.165-166

Ex. 5.41 The melodic shapes of mm. 157-158 and mm. 165-166

In measures 171-172 the left hand resumes the iambic rhythm as before (measures 63-64), toward the C-sharp minor section, which can be considered a parallel of F minor one in measure 65. At measure 173, the ballade reaches a new climax; the left hand continues the same rhythmic feature, while the right hand highlights the melodic contour of the F minor section. It raises the intensity by means of broken octaves and thickened texture. In addition, the rhythmic complexity in the F minor section has gone; however this simplicity gives the appearance of strength, expressing even the melody in *fortissimo*.

Ex. 5.42 mm.173-176

Followed by a long circle of fifths while maintaining the same texture, the tonality is finalized in E major with B dominant pedal tone in the left hand. The right hand performs an accented B, preparing for the second theme in E major, with the grumbling left-hand tremolo, presenting a broken octave on B with a half-step-down A-sharp to create an anxious moment. Accented by *sf* on the first eighths, the second eighths of B are tied; rhythmically they are articulated by the surprising A-sharp on the down beat of the left hand:

111

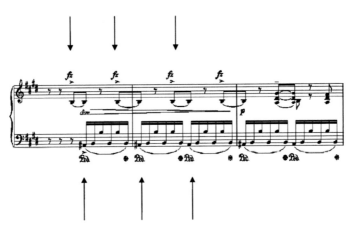

Ex. 5.43 mm. 183-185

Chopin seems to love a section of anxiety and uncertainty in terms of rhythm and tonality to prepare the coda. In the second ballade, he does this in a similar manner with a tremolo figure in the right hand:

Ex. 5.44 mm.157-161, the second ballade

As in the second ballade, in the third ballade we have 26 measures of preparation, yet we don't have a clue where Chopin will lead us, because the tonality keeps changing step by step. The first one is in E major; after a chromatic scale in the left hand while the right hand hits the first unexpected C-natural following the first B-flat; now the key modulates to F major. With the same manner, Chopin leads us to G minor; but this time the transition becomes shorter and goes straight to the home key of A-flat. During the process of key changes, the left hand always keeps the dominant pedal tones underneath; the rhythm remains intact, and the right hand introduces the first theme from the second theme:

Ex. 5.45 mm.183-193

After four-measures of chromatic ascending octaves in the right hand with the left-hand's nervous sixteenths, astonishing E-flat pedals and alternating lower and upper accented A-flat and C-flat, there comes the glorious elaboration of the first theme, just as in the similar passages in the G minor Ballade (m.106) and the Barcarolle (m.93), including octaves in the right hand and full chords in the left hand. Instead of copying the first theme, Chopin gives himself freedom to alter the details of the rhythm and melody:

mm.214-216

mm.219-222

Ex. 5.46 mm. 214-216 and mm. 219-222

The first alternation in measures 215 and 216 highlights the F—E-flat motive and contains rhythmically straightforward eighths followed by a breath of a sixteenth rest for the next phrase:

Ex. 5.47 The F—E-flay motive in m. 216

The second alternation creates a leap of melodic contour followed by the F—E-flat motive with the steady eighths. Once again the locations of the motive are at the weak beat, just as in the left hand passage in measures 157-164:

Ex. 5.48 The F—E-flat motive in m. 220

The third alternation explores more wildly with bigger leaps and half-steps moving chromatically downward followed by agitated rests and sixteenth upbeats:

Ex. 5.49 mm. 212-214

This particular melody, fragmented by sixteenth rests, makes two melodic voices from one, while the frequent rests heat up the atmosphere and keep the passion toward the stretto in measure 227. Harmonically the bass moves from E-flat to B chromatically, supporting the crazy jumping between two melodic voices in the right hand. As far as the B dominant chord in measure 225, the heat hasn't stopped yet. Using the divided-oriented melodic shape between the two hands, Chopin reaches the tonic chord with the C on top. Although the

114

harmonic changes keep the passage busy, rhythmically there is a force to push up the eighths towards the final end—from measure 221 the D-flat is waiting for six measures to reach its destination C in measure 227:

Ex. 5.50 The melodic outline of mm. 221-227

The return of the A-flat major chord is not the end of the journey but a turning point of the continuation. Chopin puts "stretto" and "crescendo" with full chords in both hands to maintain the heat. With the two strong E-flat basses, Chopin sets up a structure of two-measure rhythmic flow. Finally, a codetta *piu mosso* enters. Following the two-measure flow set-up in the previous phrase, Chopin repeats the material from measure 116:

mm.116-117

mm.231-232

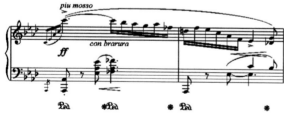

Ex. 5.51 mm. 116-117 and mm. 231-232

Instead of starting from E-flat, Chopin hammers the C from the beginning of the arpeggios:

Ex. 5.52 The arpeggios in m. 231 and m. 235

115

In measure 235, the ornamented arpeggio figure is given a rhythmic context supported by the left-hand Waltz rhythm, emphasizing the tenth from C to E-flat. The trills on the E-flat with the dissonance D-natural, as well as the left hand accompaniment, display a strong iambic rhythm:

Ex. 5.53 mm. 235-236

The final virtuoso flourish across the keyboard includes the F—E-flat motive in every octave. After a two-measure arpeggio down to the low A-flat, Chopin ends the piece with a beautiful cadence containing the last appearance of the F—E-flat motive, accented in the bass in octaves. The chords are arranged in a straightforward pulse.

Ex. 5.54 The melodic outline of the last five measures

Narrative and the Form

According to the discussion above, the rhythmic gestures in Chopin's third ballade are influenced by the rhythm of Adam Mickiewicz's *Świtezianka*. The motivic shape, introduced in the first theme, is of a trochaic motion that is often used in *Świtezianka* as a symbol of falling. Falling is a natural motion of relaxation and dragging, and commonly it is used to symbolize the feeling of melancholy. In Mickiewicz's ballads the supernatural plays an important role; therefore, the supernatural power provides another icon of falling. Since the topics of love and supernatural control are present in Mickiewicz's ballads, the falling motive is also an important symbolic figure in the three other Chopin ballades.

Although in the metrical view, the motives seems to be of an iambic motion, according to the influence of other musical effects, the performance of those motives follows a trochaic motion. The first theme of the first ballade starts on an upbeat and forms an arc of melodic shaping. Since the harmonization of this melodic fragment moves strongly from the dominant chord with a B-flat suspension on the peak of the melodic line resolving to a G minor tonic, there is a tension followed by a relief—from a strong upbeat to a weak downbeat. This example shows the creation of a falling motion initiating from a weak beat in capturing "a strong falling in powerlessness and alienation", a device that Chopin often used. Not only is the idea of powerlessness in his life mentioned by Dorota Zakrzewska, but within powerlessness, a strong theme of love, punishment, and tragic failure and loss in Mickiewicz's ballads inspired Chopin to write his ballades:

Ex. 5.55 The falling motion in the first theme of the first ballade

Similar gestures of falling motion occur in all four of Chopin's ballades Jim Samson utters "the unity of form and expression" to describe the analogy of the melodic and rhythmic contour in the themes (p. 122 in Chapter V), the falling figures generally occurring on the weak beat. While we have a steady metric flow in the left hand underneath those trochaic figures, there are playful polyrhythms between them.

The polyrhythm is frequently used in Chopin's ballades. Besides the trochaic figure performed on the weak beat to make an implication of metric shift, the intensity generated by the hemiole is also found in his ballades (pp. 137-139 in Chapter V). Within the steadiness of a periodic framework, the irregularity of rhythmic activities provokes the mood of uncertainty and disorientation. In poetry, the combinations of amphibrach and iambic feet, along with other ones, create a polyrhythmic effect as well. In Mickiewicz's ballads, within the periodic four phrases as grouped in a stanza, there are alternations between two different types of rhyme and meter (see Fig. 5.1). Taking the first stanza of Mickiewicz's *Świtezianka* as an example (Fig. 5.4), the first line shows a feeling of stability because of the balance of 5+5 couple meter and the match between the feet and the meter. However, the second line gives us an unbalanced hemiola because of the unevenness of the 3+2+3 triple meter against the flow of a couple meter which is set up in advance (Fig. 5.5). In addition, the combinations of trochee and amphibrach feet create a metric shift where the unstressed syllable is on the metric pulse (Fig. 5.6):

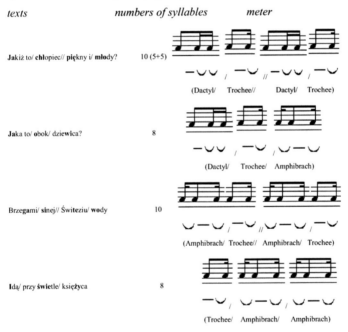

Fig. 5.4 The meter and the number of syllables in the first stanza of *Świtezianka*

Fig. 5.5 Above: meter in the second line. Below: metric flow set up in the first line

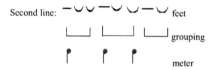

Fig. 5.6 The polyrhythm between grouping and meter in the second line

On the other hand, the effect of the weak syllable on the metric pulse is also found in the waltz sections of Chopin's first, third, and fourth ballades. Unlike the regular waltz, in which the rhythmic accent is always on the first beat, Chopin alters the design of the waltz rhythm, by lifting the first beat in the bass with a delightful staccato, followed by an accented second beat with a slur connecting to the third. With the effects of virtuosic flourishes in the right hand, the waltz becomes a unique passage of cheerfulness in contradiction to the whole ballade.

The author has discovered that aside from the connection between the rhythmic structure of Chopin's ballades and the prosody of Mickiewicz's ballads, Chopin's ballades are also formalized by the influence of poetic form. The process unfolds in a three-part development, reflected in the form of Chopin's balldes. David Buchan's study in *The Ballad and the Folk* argues that the narrative characteristic of patterning has a purpose of creating variety for repetitions. Buchan writes in *The Ballad and the Folk* that in most of the ballades "the central action is developed in three steps" (p. 114). We observe this clearly in both *Świtezianka* and Chopin's third ballade. The central action of the poetry starts from the conversations between the hunter and the nymph. They first meet, become attracted to each other, and then the nymph asks for an oath from the hunter that "he could love her no matter what". This is the first step. The second step shows the hunter wandering in the woods, who, after meeting a beautiful maid—actually the nymph but in different appearance—, forgets about his oath and instantly falls in love with the new maid. In the second step, the same characters transform into different shapes; the hunter loses his faithfulness to the nymph who transforms her appearance to test the hunter's loyalty. Unfortunately, the hunter falls in love with the maid's beauty, unawaring that it is a trap created by the nymph. Finally, in the third step the two characters discover the truth; the hunter realizes that the maid he meets is the nymph, and the nymph figures out that her love is never pure.

Just as the structure of *Świtezianka*, the central action of Chopin's third ballade also unfolds in the second part, divided into three steps as well. The second theme repeats three times in three different combinations: the first step is the first statement of the second theme, followed by a transforming F minor section. In the second step, a new third theme is added after the recapitulation of the second theme. The third step conjoins the first and the second themes and Chopin generates more complicated textures in terms of harmony and rhythm in creating an atmosphere of anxiety and conflict. In addition, the structure of each step shows an iambic shape: the introductory section of the second theme functions as a structural upbeat toward the longer main sections—F minor in the first step, A-flat waltz in the second step, and the C-sharp minor in the third:

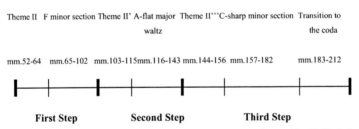

Theme II F minor section Theme II' A-flat major Theme II'''C-sharp minor section Transition to
waltz   the coda

mm.52-64   mm.65-102   mm.103-115mm.116-143 mm.144-156 mm.157-182   mm.183-212

First Step   **Second Step**   **Third Step**

Fig. 5.7 The three-step development in the central part of the third ballade

The three-step development can be observed in smaller episodes as well. The waltz is developed in three parts: the first is a showcase of ornamented arpeggios in the right hand with iambic melodic figures in the left hand; the second presents a long virtuoso passage of the right hand with a steady iambic waltz rhythm in the accompaniment; in the last, with the left hand's arpeggiated accompaniment, the melody shows the remembrance of the F—E-flat motive from the first theme. Another example is located in the transition part which connects to the coda. From measure 183, the tonality changes chromatically three times, and the energy gradually increases in three levels toward the climax of the piece.

Here in *Świtezianka* the nymph and the hunter appear in three different situations. In each situation Mickiewicz always begins with a stanza illustrating the hunter walking nearby the water and encountering the nymph, but in three different appearances: the first in an original look, the second with a fake exterior, and the third with anger and punishment. The three-step development in Mickiewicz's ballads can be observed in the other Chopin's ballades as well. The first theme of the first ballades is repeated three times in different styles—the second one is in A minor which is a whole step up from the original tonality, and the third one displays an incomplete version with a bridge to the coda:

The original statement of the first theme:

Second time in A minor:

Third time with a bridge:

Ex. 5.56 The three different thematic variations in the first ballade

The first theme of the fourth ballade appears three times, but the latter two are more rhythmically and harmonically complex than the first one:

The original statement of the first theme:

The second time:

The third time:

Ex. 5.57 The three different thematic variations in the fourth ballade

However, the second ballade is of a unique type of thematic variations compared with the other three ballades. In this case, inspired by the story of Mickiewicz's *Świteź*, there is a comparative temporal contrast between the past and the present. The Polish maidens, who become flowers on the shores of the lake *Świteź*, were swallowed by the water of *Świteź*—a sacrifice for their people in order to escape from the hands of conquerors. Therefore, the spirits of those maidens stay in the flowers, and, whoever touches them will be cursed. A calm lake with beautiful but mysterious flowers in the present is haunted by a tragic past. Hence, in the music the first theme is stated in the introduction but ends on a puzzle, exemplified by repeating A's in the right hand. Following the powerful contrast of the second theme, the first theme comes out, although this time it is much shorter than the first time. The third appearance of the theme delays until the last moment, presented in a completely new key—A minor. Therefore, the ending, utilizing the key of the dramatic second theme (A minor) as opposed to the home key (F major), evokes a memory of the past —the Polish maidens sacrificed for their people in the war:

The first theme with an ending of repeating A:

The second time:

The third time (The ending):

Ex. 5.58 The three different thematic variations in the second ballade

Here we present a significant implication concerning the accepted notion that, from the musical standpoint, the form of the Chopin ballades is a derivative of sonata form. Jim Samson believes that Chopin deviates in fascinating ways from the conventions of sonata form (*Chopin: the Four Ballades*, p. 56) and transforms it. He divides the third ballade into three parts based on the structure of traditional sonata form: the exposition section (mm. 1-115), the development (mm. 144-212), and the recapitulation (mm. 213-241). The gap between the exposition and the development sections and the last part of the development (mm. 183-212) are considered Chopin's reinterpretation of the normative functions of sonata form. From measure 116 Chopin presents an independent episode which remains in the home key but possesses none of the qualities of a development section. Chopin creates a new waltz and develops it in three parts to provide a contrast to the first and the second themes, and it forms the central pinnacle of a formal arch, flanked by the exposition and the mirror reprise (Samson, *Chopin: the Four Ballades* p. 61). Another section which is unusual in this derivation from the sonata form is in the last part of the development. Chopin makes a thematic circle via a chromatic sequence. Chopin's thematic treatment is unique in that, for the first time in this piece, he merges the first and the second themes into a single melodic line.

Another possible proposal in interpreting the form of this ballade is that it constitutes a kind of rondo (Neil Witten, pp. 347-355) by attributing the same function to the two themes with an additional third theme. According to Witten, the combination of stable areas and developmental digressions allows this piece to be convincingly considered as a rondo (p. 347):

A---digression---(A)---B---digression---B---digression---A---coda
Measure: 1   9   (37) 54 116   146 183   213 231

Fig. 5.8 A rondo structure proposed by Neil Witten

However, unlike the conventional rondo, the recurring thematic areas are divided into two contrasting themes, and only the A theme remains in the tonic key; the B theme appears in the submediant and subdominant. While the ballade resembles a rondo, the recurring areas of stability are equivalent only thematically; they are varied in tonality, texture, and rhythmic gestures. This is exemplary of Chopin's inconsistency in embrasing the conventional forms but reconstructing them in the spirit of the nineteenth-century Romanticism. Regarding the digressions between thematic areas, the first two digressions are more stable than the third one, since both begin in the tonic key. The third digression, however, the most unstable

124

one—developed via sequences of tonal alternation, reveals the identical nature of the A and the B themes perfectly within a single melodic shape.

Both Samson and Witten view the ballades through purely musical considerations, yet this researcher has richer and more cogent interpretation revealed the original idea of Chopin's creation if we evaluate the form of Chopin's ballades by a setting originated from that of poetic ballads. Although like sonata form, it is still ternary, unlike a development section the central part is the longest and the most active and developed by a three-step format. In order to demonstrate the ballade as a musical narrative form, therefore, the terminology used in the formal analysis of Chopin's third ballade below is borrowed from that of dramatic settings (Fig. 5.9).

As mentioned in the beginning of this chapter, ballads usually present contrasts with balances, antitheses, appositions, and parallelisms in two-part structure, and make repetitions in three-part structure. The repetitions are seldom the same, but more often they are repetitions with variation each time. In Świtezianka, the story can be divided into three acts. The first one is an introduction of the happening event—where and how the two characters meet, and the hint that they are attracted to each other. The second one is the longest and the center of the story, in which the dialogue between the nymph and the hunter begin, while the narrator interrupts to introduce the next scenario. The last stage is the revenge of the nymph; after she turns back into her previous form, she punishes the hunter for his discretion of unfaithfulness. Finally, in the last two stanzas the surroundings change back to those from the beginning of the poem. The last two stanzas essentially echo the first three, but unlike the naivety of the first part, the conclusion seems to hint at something that had happened before. Intentionally, Mickiewicz uses the past tense in the third line of the last stanza, "Któż jest młodzieniec? - strzelcem był w borze" (Who was the youth? A hunter in the forest[6]).

Reflected in Chopin's third ballade, he utilizes a powerful return of the first theme combined with an echo of the third theme in the second act, not only to summarize the themes introduced in the previous acts, but to transform them with variations of melodic shapes, rhythms, and phrase extensions. The first and the third themes appear in contrast between the first and the last acts, in which a symmetrical form as a whole is constructed. Furthermore, in the central part of the piece, the second theme is repeated twice in parallel major-minor tonalities, both in the first and the third steps. However, as Parakilas mentions,

---

[6] Translated by Krzysztof Sobolewski.

	First Act (Introduction)	Second (Central) Act (Action)							Third (Coda)	Act
		First Scene (Step 1)		Second Scene (Step 2)			Third Scene (Step 3)			
	m.1	m.52	m.65	m.103	m.116	m.144	m.157	m.183	m.213	m.231
	First Theme	Second Theme	Variation of Second Theme	Recap of Second theme	Third Theme	Recap of Second Theme	Variation of Second Theme	Junction of First and Second Theme	First Theme	Third Theme
	A-flat Major	F Major	F Minor	F Major	A-flat Major	D-flat Major	C-sharp Minor	Modulatory	A-flat Major	A-flat Major

Fig. 5.9 The overall structure of the third ballade suggested by the author

the repetition is not the same. In the first step the repeated second theme is transformed into the key of F minor, and the texture is thickened by the addition of chords and octaves. After the recap of the second theme, it modulates to an anxious area in the key of C-sharp minor featuring more rapid rhythmic figures in the third step.

Both Samson's and Witten's observations are purely musical. However, in this researcher's analyzing the structure of the ballades by comparison to the literary ballads, as the example of Chopin's third ballade and *Świtezianka* in the fifth chapter, we can see that Chopin's third ballade is basically in a ternary form with a longer and most active second part. His other ballades, although most of the scholars suggest that they are formalized according to the sonata form, are also of three-part form with an active and weighted central part. The first and the fourth ballades initiate a short eight-measure introduction, and the central section emanates from the first statement of the first theme, developing in three steps with other thematic materials. Conversely, the second and the third ballades begin with the first theme, while the center is the development section of the second and the third themes.

Therefore, we cannot explain the form of the ballades based on conventional musical forms, because the structure of the ballades unfolds in a continuous development analogous to the narrative format of poetic ballads. It can be said that Chopin invented a new form for his ballades, a "ballad" form appropriated from the most popular form of storytelling, whereas the central action of the story follows a short introduction, and the story completes itself with a dramatic ending. In *Świtezianka*, the narrator introduces the characters in the first section, the second section begins the main scenes of the story, and finally, the story reaches the climax in the last —finished by an echo of the opening scene. To conclude, Chopin's third ballade gives us a model of musical narrative by imitating the literary narrative, in which he follows the form of Mickiewicz's ballad, a popular device for constructing a form of narrative.

CONCLUSION

This study provides an alternative analytical approach for Chopin's ballades. Recent articles and dissertations regarding Chopin's ballades concentrate on the study of harmonic and melodic structures, although some of them refer to their relationship with Mickiewicz's poetic ballads. Dorota Zakrzewska's study on Chopin's second ballade demonstrates the influences of personal and social backgrounds on the music and the poetry based on the similarity of expression in musical and poetic themes and textures. Jim Samson's study in his book *Chopin: The Four Ballades* offers a general investigation of all musical elements and structures as well as the social and cultural influences beyond the music. In addition, Keefer Lubov's article "The Influence of Adam Mickiewicz on the Ballades of Chopin" views the melodic and harmonic structures, as well as the thematic relationships and the form, as connections to Mickiewicz's poems.

However, this study proffers the connection with Mickiewicz's ballads as rooted in the rhythmic shapes and structures of Chopin's ballades, as more directly corresponding to those of Mickiewicz's verses. Most scholars would not dispute the fact that the Chopin's ballades have strong rhythmic characteristics, since most of them discuss rhythm in terms of unified sextuple meters. The concentration on harmonic and melodic structures in Chopin's ballades, however, is found throughout the scholarly literature, largely due to Chopin's beautiful, complex, and intriguing treatment of those elements—a worthy endeavor. However, this study proves that rhythm, although commonly disregarded, is also a crucial element in forming a narrative style in a sense of temporal development created by the arrangement of meters, stresses, and formal elements, i.e. the length of phrases, the nature and amount of phrases and sections, or the repetition of motives. In addition, not only is a literary association to the ballade revealed, according to the historical finding, but the ballade is also one of the earliest song-forms in accompanying dance—generating strong rhythmic characters associated with the physical movements of human beings. As a result, through an analysis of rhythm, the performers may interpret the ballades with an awareness of the rhythmic characteristics originated in the ballades as well as their connection to poetry.

Other musical aspects, such as melodic and harmonic shapes and structures, are highly relevant in a rhythmic analysis, because those elements affect the rhythmic design. For instance, a melodic shape can influence the duration of notes and change the style of motion from one note to another. As we can see in the discussion of the trochaic motive in chapter V, the pitches, directed from higher to lower ranges, display a motion of falling owing to a natural emphasis on the higher pitch. Analogously, as we speak, we tend to lengthen the duration of the word if we wish it to be emphasized. Therefore, as Cooped and Meyer indicate, musical tensions and releases are influenced by the melodic and harmonic structures as well as the organization of texture and form, thereby shaping the grouping of rhythmic shapes and structures. In addition, the philosophy of Langer and Kivy supports the significance of expressiveness in rhythmic shapes and temporal developments which demonstrate an association between musical gestures and emotional and philosophical contexts.

William Rothstein illustrates a stanzaic and metrical analysis of the themes of three ballades in his article "Ambiguity in the Themes of Chopin's First, Second, and Fourth Ballades". Although he shows the connection between the rhythmic groupings of the themes of Chopin's ballades and the feet of Mickiewicz's ballads, Rothstein's approach toward rhythmic analysis is intrinsic and musical. However, this study demonstrates the significance of expressiveness in rhythm in disclosing the notion of narrative. Both music and poetry have a sense of temporal movement since they are constructed via patterns of sound through time and temporal development by the arrangement of elements and texture. The groupings of sound and of temporal development express a sense of poetic and emotional flow, which forms a style of narrative—a fundamental trait of Romanticism since the late seventeenth century. The author asserts that rhythm is the essential element for evaluating the style of narrative, and analyzing rhythm is a significant device in evoking the connections between music and poetry. These relationships existed since Medieval times, when the song-forms, such as ballades and chansons, were written for minstrels and the value of personal expression and inspiration in music proclaimed the poetic and philosophical influences from poetry, folklore, history, and exotic cultures.

Furthermore, the link between Chopin and Mickiewicz's ballades/ballads is not only metrical but also formal. This study makes an innovative argument about the formal structure of Chopin's ballades. Most scholars, including Rothstein, would consider that the Chopin's ballades bear reference to sonata form, although this sonata form may be irregular. Nevertheless, this study presents an alternative point of view that the formal setting of the ballades tends to be formalized in a ballad form, by which the most weighted and important portion is located at the center of the ballade, essentially deriving from the model of poetic ballads. Unlike the impact of harmonic progressions in the structure of sonata form, the structure of ballad form is constructed by continuous thematic transformations, developed by alternative rhythmic and harmonic structures—an imitation of a continuous transformation of themes and situations in poetic ballads.

As we evaluate rhythm in this study, the inventiveness of Chopin encompasses the emotional statement. Not only does he create a new setting of form as a reflection of poetic ballads, his compositions broaden the horizons of musical expression by demonstrating profound experience and tragedy, as well as encompassing new energy states of heroic euphoria and romantic fantasy. They disclose the subtle nuance of moods, going far beyond the expressive conventions of his time. Indeed, Chopin exerted a tremendous impact on the development of piano music and provided a foundation for the piano works of his contemporaries and for the later generations of Scriabin, Debussy, Ravel, and Rachmaninoff.

To conclude, Chopin's ballades give an impression of developing a narrative which reflects Mickiewicz's ballads. By analyzing the poetic and emotional meanings of their rhythmic gestures and structures, we discover that they accomplish a synthesis of both a distinct ethnic color of expression and a convention of musical effects—transformed by the composer in his own fashion by aiming at reflecting his fellow's poetic works. Filled with fantastic, dramatic moods, these works develop assorted emotional motives that illustrate a style of narrative, each depicting a supreme tension and emotional relief toward the climax of a turbulent coda, similar to the endings in poetic ballads. By the observation of rhythm in relationship to its literary influence, this alternative approach toward the Chopin ballades hold significant implications for performance practices.

BIBLIOGRAPHY

Books:

Abbate, Carolyn. *Unsung Voices: Opera and Musical Narrative in the Nineteenth Century.*
Princeton: Princeton UP, 1991.

Abraham, Gerald. *Chopin's Musical Style.* London: Oxford UP, 1960.

Aiello, Rita, and John A Sloboda, ed. *Musical Perceptions.* Oxford UP, 1996.

Atwood, William G. *Fryderyk Chopin: Pianist from Warsaw.* New York: Columbia UP, 1987

———. *The Parisian Worlds of Frédéric Chopin.* New Haven: Yale UP, 1999.

Bonds, Mark Evan. *Wordless Rhetoric: Musical Form and the Metaphor of the Oration.*

Branson, David. *John Field and Chopin.* New York: St. Martin's Press, 1972.

Buchan, David. *The Ballade and the Folk.* London: Routledge & Kegan Paul, 1972.

Burrows, David. *Sound, Speech, and Music.* The Univ. of Massachusetts P, 1990.

Chomiński, Józef M. *Chopin.* Kraków: Polskie Wydawnictwo Muzyczne, 1978.

Chopin, Fryderyk. *Ballades.* In *Complete Works* Vol. 3. Ed. I. J. Paderewski, L. Bronarski,
and J. Turczyski. Kraków: Instytut Fryderyka Chopina and Polskie Wydawnictwo
Muzyczne, 1986.

Cogan, Robert, and Pozzi Esot. *Sonic Design: The Nature of Sound and Music.* Englewood
Cliffs, NJ: Prentice Hall, 1976.

131

Coleman, Marion M. *Adam Mickiewicz in English 1827-1955*. Cambridge Springs: Alliance College, 1954.

Coker, Wilson. *Music and Meaning*. Free P, 1972.

Cooke, Deryck. *The Language of Music*. New York: Oxford UP, 1959.

Cooper, Grosvenor, and Lenard B. Meyer. *The Rhythmic Structure of Music*. Chicago: The Univ. of Chicago P, 1960.

Dahlhaus, Carl. *Nineteenth-Century Music*. Trans. by J. Bradford Robinson. Univ. of California P, 1989.

Ehrlich, Cyril. *The Piano: A History*. Clarendon P, 1990.

Eigeldinger, Jean-Jacques. *Chopin: Pianist and Teacher*. Trans. Naomi Scohet, ed. Roy Howat, Cambridge: Cambridge UP, 1986.

Einstein, Alfred. *Music in the Romantic Era*. New York: W. W. Norton, 1947.

Eisler, Benita. *Chopin's Funeral*. New York: Alfred A. Knopf, Random House, Inc., 2003.

Erlich, Victor. *Russian Formalism*. Mouton de Gruyter, 1980

Ferrara, Lawrence. *Philosophy and the Analysis of Music: Bridges to Musical Sound, Form, and Reference*. Excelsior Music Pub., 1991.

Gabrielsson, Alf, ed. *Action and Perception in Rhythm and Music*. Publications issued by the Royal Swedish Academy of Music No.55, 1987.

Gould, Gordon H. *The Ballad of Tradition*. Oxford UP, 1932.

Grove, George. *Beethoven and His Nine Symphonies*. Dover, 1962.

132

Hanslick, Eduard. *Music Criticisms 1846-1899*. Trans. Henry Pleasants. Baltimore: Pelican
   Books, 1963.

Hedley, Arthur, ed. *Selected Correspondence of Frédéric Chopin*. London: McGraw-Hill
   Book Company, 1963.

Hindley, Geoffrey, ed., *The Larousse Encyclopedia of Music*. Chancellor P, 1997.

Hoffman, Michael J., and Patrick D. Murphy, ed. *Essentials of the Theory of Fiction*. Duke
   UP, 1988

Holcman, Jan. *The Legacy of Chopin*. New York: Philosophical Library, 1954.

Hoppin, Richard H. *Medieval Music*. W. W. Norton & Company, 1978.

Huneker, James Gibbons. *Chopin: The Man and His Music*. Dover, 1966.

Langer, Susanne K. *Philosophy in a New Key: A Study in the Symbolism of Reason, Rite, and
   Arts*. New York: Mentor Books, 1959.

———. *Feeling and Form: A Theory of Art Developed from Philosophy in a New Key*. New
   York: Charles Scribner's Sons, 1953.

Leeuwen, Theo van. *Speech, Music, Sound*. New York: St. Martin's P, 1999.

Lentricchia, Frank, and Thomas MacLaughlin, ed. *Critical Terms for Literary Study*. Chicago:
   The Univ. of Chicago P, 1990.

Lester, Joel. *The Rhythms of Tonal Music*. Carbondale: Southern Illinois UP, 1986.

Liszt, Franz. *Frédéric Chopin*. Trans. Martha Walker Cook. Boston: Oliver Ditson, 1863.

Karasowski, Moritz. *Frederic Chopin: His Life and Letters*. Trans. Emily Hill. Greenwood P, 1938.

Kelley, Edgar Stillman. *Chopin the Composer: His Structural Art and Its Influence on Contemporaneous Music*. New York: G. Schirmer, 1913.

Kivy, Peter. *Sound and Semblance: Reflections on Musical Representation*. Princeton, N.J.: Princeton UP, 1984.

———. *Sound Sentiment: An Essay on the Musical Emotions, including the Complete Text of "The Corded Shell*. Philadelphia: Temple UP, 1989.

———. *Music Alone*. Cornell UP, 1990.

———. *Introduction to a Philosophy of Music*. Oxford UP, 2002.

Koch, Heinrich Christoph. *Introductory Essay on Composition: The Mechanical Rules of Melody, Sections 3 and 4*. Trans. Nancy Kovaleff Baker. New Haven: Yale UP, 1983.

Kramer, Lawrence. *Music and Poetry: The Nineteenth Century and After*. Berkeley: Univ. of California P, 1984.

———. *Music as Cultural Practice, 1800-1900*. Berkeley: Univ. of California P, 1990.

Kridl, Manfred, ed. *Adam Mickiewicz: Poet of Poland*. New York: Greenwood P, 1969.

Methuen-Campbell, James. *Chopin Playing from the Composer to the Present Day*. London: Victor Gollancz, 1981.

Meyer, Leonard B. *Music, the Arts, and Ideas: Patterns and Predictions in Twentieth-Century Culture*. The Univ. of Chicago P, 1967.

Mickiewicz, Adam. *Selected Poetry and Prose*. Ed. Stanisaw Helsztyski, trans. George Rapall Noyes, and Jewell Parish. Warsaw: Polonia Publishing House, 1955.

————. *The Sun of Liberty*. Ed. Michael J. Mikoś, trans. Wydawnictwo Energeia, 1998.

————. *Selection of Poems in Five Centuries of Polish Poetry 1450-1970*, 2nd ed. Jerzy Peterkiewicz and Burns Singer, ed. Westport: Greenwood P, 1979.

————. *Poems*. Trans. Jack Lindsay. London: Sylvan P, 1957.

————. *Poems by Adam Mickiewicz*. Trans. and ed. by George Rapall Noyes. New York: The Polish Institute of Arts and Sciences in America, 1944.

Nattiez, Jean Jacques. *Music and Discourse: Toward a Semiology of Music*. Trans. Carolyn Abbate. Princeton: Princeton UP, 1990.

Opieński, H, ed. *Chopin's Letters*. Trans. E. L. Voynich. New York: Dover, 1931, rev. 1971.

Parakilas, James. *Ballads Without Words: Chopin and the Tradition of the Instrumental Ballade*. Portland, Oregon: Amadeus P, 1992.

Phelps, P. Roger, Lawrence Ferrara, and Thomas W. Goolsby. *A Guide to Research in Music Education*. Metuchen, NJ: The Scarecrow P, 1993.

Perkins, Leeman L. *Music in the Age of the Renaissance*. W. W. Norton & Company, 1999.

Preminger, Alex, ed. *Princeton Encyclopedia of Poetry and Poetics*. Enlarged ed., Princeton, New Jersey: Princeton UP, 1974.

Propp, Vladimir. *Morphology of the Folktale*. Univ. of Texas P, 1968.

Ratner, Leonard. *Classical Music: Expression, Form, and Style*. New York: Schirmer Books, 1980.

Rosen, Charles. *The Romantic Generation*. Harvard UP, 1995.

Rothstein, William. *Phrase Rhythm in Tonal Music*. New York: Schirmer Books, 1989.

Sadie, Stanley, and George Grove, ed. *The New Grove Dictionary of Music and Musicians*. Grove's Dictionaries, Inc., 1981.

Samson, Jim. *Chopin: The Four Ballades*. Cambridge: Cambridge UP, 1992.

———. *Chopin*. Schirmer Books, 1996.

———. *The Music of Chopin*. London: Routledge & Kegan
Paul Pub., 1985.

———, ed. *The Cambridge Companion to Chopin*. Cambridge: Cambridge UP, 1992.

Schonberg, H.C. *The Great Pianists from Mozart to the Present*. Simon and Schuster,
1963.

Schumann, Robert. *On Music and Musicians*. Trans. Paul Rosenfeld. New York: Norton,
1969.

Siepmann, Jeremy. *Chopin: The Reluctant Romantic*. Boston: Northeastern UP, 1995.

Sorantin, Erich. *The Problem of Musical Expression: A Philosophical and Psychological
Study*. Nashville, Tennessee: Marshall & Bruce Co., 1932.

Strunk, Oliver. *Source Readings in Music History*. New York: Norton, 1950.

Szulc, Tad. *Chopin in Paris*. New York: Da Capo P, 1998.

Walicki, Andrzej. *Philosophy and Romantic Nationalism: The Case of Poland*. Oxford:
Clarendon P, 1982.

Weintraub, Wiktor. *The Poetry of Adam Mickiewicz*. Mouton & Co, 1954.

Welsh, David. *Adam Mickiewicz*. New York: Twayne Publishers, 1966.

Zebrowski, Dariusz, ed. *Studies in Chopin*. Warsaw: The Chopin society, 1973.

136

Dissertations:

Almen, Byron Paul. *Narrative Archetypes in Music: A Semiotic Approach.* Diss. Indiana
Univ., 1998. Ann Arbor: UMI, 1998. 9834583.

Dabrusin, Ross. *Deriving Structural Motives: Implications for Music Performance.* Diss.
New York Univ., 1995. Ann Arbor: UMI, 1995. 9528283.

Enlow, Charles Alva Jr. *The Thirteen Barcarolles for Piano by Gabriel Faure: An Analytical
and Interpretive Study.* Diss. the Univ. of Texas at Austin, 2000. Ann Arbor: UMI, 2001.
3004199.

Friedman, Michael. *Sorrow as A Reflection of Chopin's Onto-historical World in the
Structure of His Melodies: Analysis and Performance Guide.* Diss. New York Univ., 2000.
Ann Arbor: UMI, 2000. 9955719.

Kallberg, Jeffery. *The Chopin Sources: Variants and Versions in Later Manuscripts
and Printed Editions.* Diss. the U of Chicago, 1982. Ann Arbor: UMI, 1983. T-28377.

Stevens, Jessica Rose. *Formal Considerations in Chopin's Last Works: Performance
Problems.* Diss. U of Washington, 1984. Ann Arbor: UMI, 1984. 8404954.

Taggart, Bruce Finley. *Rhythmic Perception and Conception: A Study of Bottom-Up and Top-
Down Interaction in Rhythm and Meter.* Diss. Univ. of Pennsylvania, 1996. Ann Arbor:
UMI, 1996. 9628012.

Trechak, Andrew, Jr. *Pianists and Agogic Play: Rhythmic Pattering in the Performance of
Chopin's Music in the Early Twentieth Century.* Diss. The Univ. of Texas at Austin,
1988. Ann Arbor: UMI, 1989. 8909777.

Turrill, Pauline Venable. "The Piano Ballade in the Romantic Era: A Categorical Study of
Styles as Suggested by Genres of Narrative Poetry." Diss. Univ. of Southern California,
1977.

Witten, Neil. "The Chopin Ballades: An Analytical Study." Diss. Boston Univ., 1974.

137

Articles:

Auclert, Pierre. "La Ballade, Op. 19 de Fauré", *Bulletin de l'Association des Amis de Gabriel Fauré* 15 (1978): 3-11.

Berger, Karol. "The Form of Chopin's Ballade, Op.23", *Nineteenth-Century Music* 20, no.1 (1996): 46-71.

Eigeldinger, Jean-Jacques. "Placing Chopin: Reflections on a Compositional Aesthetic", *Chopin Studies* 2, ed. J. Rink and J. Samson, Cambridge, 1994, p.102-139.

Friedman, Albert B. "Ballad", *Encyclopedia Britannica: Macropedia*, 15th ed., vol. 2. Chicago: Encyclopedia Britannica, Inc., 1974, pp. 641-645.

Hedley, Arthur. "Some Notes on Chopin Biography", *Music and Letters* Vol.18, no.1 (1937): 42-49.

Holland, Jeanne. "Chopin's Piano Method", *The Piano Quarterly*, No. 129 (Spring 1985): 32-43.

Jarecki, Tadeusz. "The Most Polish of Polish Composers", *Frederick Chopin: 1810-1849*, ed. Stephen P. Mizwa, The Macmillan Company, 1949.

Keefer, Lubov. "The Influence of Adam Mickiewicz on the Ballades of Chopin", *American Slavic and East European Review* Vol.5 (1946): 38-50.

Kramer, Lawrence. "Musical Narratology: A Theoretical Outline", *Indiana Theory Review* 12 (1991): 141-162.

Kramer, Richard. "Notes to Beethoven's Education", *Journal of the American Musicological Society,* vol. 28, 1975, pp. 72-101.

Maus, Fred Everett. "Music as Narrative", *Indiana Theory Review 12* (1991): *1-34.*

Newcomb, Anthony. "Schumann and Late Eighteenth-Century Narrative Strategies", *Nineteenth-Century Music* 11, no.2 (1987): 164-174.

———. "One More 'Between Absolute and Program Music.': Schumann's Second Symphony", *Nineteenth-Century Music* 7 (1984): 233-250.

———. "Narrative Strategies in Nineteenth-Century Instrumental Music", *Music and Text: Critical Inquiries*. Steven Paul Scher, ed. Cambridge, 1992.

Reaney, Gilbert. "Concerning the Origins of the Rondeau, Virelai, and Ballade Forms", *Musica Disciplina* Vol.6 (1952): 155-166.

Ritter, Rüdiger. "Mickiewicz and Music", *Sendung and Dichtung: Adam Mickiewicz in Europe*, ed. Zdzislaw Krasnodebski and Stefan Garsztecki. Hamburg: Reinhold Krämer Verlag, 2002.

Rothstein, William. "Ambiguity in the Themes of Chopin's First, Second, and Fourth Ballades." *Intégral* 8 (1995): 1-50.

Samson, Jim. "Chopin and Genre", *Music Analysis* Vol.8 (1989): 213-231.

Tomaszewski, Mieczysław. "Fryderyk Chopin", *Encyklopedia Muzyczna: Cz Biograficzna*. Ed. Elżbieta Dziębowska. Kraków: Polskie Wydawnictwo Muzyczne, 1984: Vol.II: 108-192.

Witten, David. "Ballads and Ballades", *The Piano Quarterly* No. 113 (Spring 1981): 33-37.

Websites:

Goldberg, Halina. "Chopin in Warsaw's Salons", *Polish Music Journal*, Vol. 2, No 1, Summer 1999: www.usc.edu/dept/polish_music/PMJ/issue/2.1.99/abstracts_2_1.html

Hasselman, Margaret P. "Songs in Fixed Forms", *The ORB: The online reference book for medieval studies*: http://the-orb.net/encyclop/culture/music/ffixe.html.

Mickiewicz, Adam. "Świtezianka", trans. by Krzysztof Sobolewski:
http://critto.webpark.pl/switezianka-en1.htm

Zakrzewska, Dorota. "Alienation and Powerlessness: Adam Mickiewicz's Ballady and
Chopin's Ballades", *Polish Music Journal* Vol. 2, No. 1, Summer 1999:
www.usc.edu/dept/polish_music/PMJ/issue/2.1.99/abstracts_2_1.html

APPENDIX

Attached is the ballad Świtezianka written by Adam Mickiewicz in 1821. The total number of stanzas is 38, with four lines in each stanza. The rhymes are alternated in the form of "abab"—the first and the third lines have the same rhyme, as the second and the fourth ones share another rhyme. The story is about a young hunter meets a maiden in the wood. She accepts his love with a promise of faithfulness. Then she leaves him and he walks homewards beside the lake. He sees another girl at the water's edge, and the fickle lover makes his way to her through the marsh. The girl is the maiden he met at the first time, the nymph of the lake. She blames him bitterly for his unfaithfulness, drags him down and drowns him. The spirit of the maiden can be seen dancing in the water, while the ghost of the hunter groans by the old larch tree.

Świtezianka

BALLADA

Jakiż to chłopiec piękny i młody?
Jaka to obok dziewica?
Brzegami sinej Świteziu wody
Idą przy świetle księżyca.
                 tide?

Who is the lad so comely and young
And who is the maid at his side
Who walk by the Switez' blue waters,
Among the moonbeams that shine on its

Ona mu z kosza daje maliny,
A on jej kwiatki do wianka;
Pewnie kochankiem jest tej dziewczyny,
Pewnie to jego kochanka.

A basket of raspberries she holds out,
He gives her a wreath for her hair;
The lad is her lover, beyond a doubt,
And she is his sweetheart fair.

Każdą noc prawie, o jednej porze,
Pod tym się widzą modrzewiem,
Młody jest strzelcem w tutejszym borze,
Kto jest dziewczyna? - ja nie wiem.

Never a night but at dusk they stand
On the shore by the old larch tree;
The youth hunts here in the forest land,
But the maiden is strange to me.

Skąd przyszła? - darmo śledzić kto pragnie;
Gdzie uszła? - nikt jej nie zbada.
Jak mokry jaskier wchodzi na bagnie,
Jak ognik nocny przepada.

You may ask in vain whence she comes and where
She vanishes: no one knows.
Like the crowfoot's moist bloom on the marsh,
She is there—like the will-o'-the-wisp, she goes.

"Powiedz mi, piękna, luba dziewczyno -
Na co nam te tajemnice -
Jaką przybiegłaś do mnie drożyną?
Gdzie dóm twój, gdzie są rodzice?

"Beautiful maid whom I love so well,
Wherefore this secrecy?
Where do your father and mother dwell,
By what road do you come to me?

" Minęło lato, zżółkniały liścia
I dżdżysta nadchodzi pora,
Zawsze mam czekać twojego przyścia
Na dzikich brzegach jeziora?

"Summer is over, the leaves grow brown,
And the rains are about to break;
Must I always wait here till you wander down
To the shore of the desolate lake?

" Zawszeż po kniejach jak sarna płocha,

"Will you range through the wood like a heedless roe,

Jak upiór błądzisz w noc ciemną?
Zostań się lepiej z tym, kto cię kocha,
Zostań się, o luba! ze mną.

Forever a ghost in the night?
Stay rather with him who will love you so,
With me, O my heart's delight!

" Chateczka moja stąd niedaleka
Po środku gęstej leszczyny;
Jest tam dostatkiem owoców, mleka,
Jest tam dostatkiem źwierzyny".

"My cottage is near where the woodland trees
Spread their sheltering branches thick;
There is plenty of milk, there is game when you please,
And the fruit from the boughs to pick."

" Stój, stój - odpowie - hardy młokosie,
Pomnę, co ojciec rzekł stary:
Słowicze wdzięki w mężczyzny głosie,
A w sercu lisie zamiary.

"Nay, have done, haughty stripling, my father's tales
Have forewarned me against your art:
For the voice of a man is the nightngale's,
But the fox's is his heart.

" Więcej się waszej obłudy boję,
Niż w zmienne ufam zapały,
Może bym prośby przyjęła twoje;
Ale czy będziesz mnie stały? "

"And I have more fear of your treachery
Than belief in your changing flame;
And were I to do what you ask of me
Would you always remain the same?"

Chłopiec przyklęknął, chwycił w dłoń piasku,
Piekielne wzywał potęgi,
Kłął się przy świętym księżyca blasku,

Then the youth knelt down and with sand in his palm
He called on the powers of hell,
He swore by the moon so holy and calm,

Lecz czy dochowa przysięgi?

Will he hold to his oath so well?

"Dochowaj, strzelcze, to moja rada:
Bo kto przysięgę naruszy,
Ach, biada jemu, za życia biada!
I biada jego złej duszy! "

"I counsel you, hunter, to keep your oath
And the promise that here you swore;
For woe to the man who shall break it, both
While he lives and forevermore."

To mówiąc dziewka więcej nie czeka,
Wieniec włożyła na skronie
I pożegnawszy strzelca z daleka,
Na zwykłe uchodzi błonie.

So saying, she places her wreath on his brow
And, making no longer stay,
She has waved him good-by from afar and now
She is over the field and away.

Próżno się za nią strzelec pomyka,
Rączym wybiegom nie sprostał,
Znikła jak lekki powiew wietrzyka,
A on sam jeden pozostał.

Vainly the hunter increases his speed,
For her fleetness outmatches his own;
She has vanished as light as the wind on the mead,
He is left on the shore alone.

Sam został, dziką powraca drogą,
Ziemia uchyla się grząska,
Cisza wokoło, tylko pod nogą
Zwiędła szeleszcze gałązka.

Alone he returns on the desolate ground
Where the marshlands heave and quake
And the air is silent—the only sound
When the dry twigs rustle and break.

Idzie nad wodą, błędny krok niesie,
Błędnymi strzela oczyma;
Wtem wiatr zaszumiał po gęstym lesie,
Woda się burzy i wzdyma.

He walks by the water with wandering tread,
He searches with wandering eyes;
On a sudden the winds through the deepwood spread
And the waters seethe and rise.

Burzy się, wzdyma, pękają tonie,
O niesłychane zjawiska !
Ponad srebrzyste Świtezi błonie
Dziewicza piękność wytryska.

They rise and the swell and their depths divide
Oh, phantoms seen only in dreams!
On the field of the Switez all silver-dyed
A beauteous maiden gleams!

Jej twarz jak róży bladej zawoje,
Skropione jutrzenki łezką;
Jako mgła lekka, tak lekkie stroje
Obwiały postać niebieską.

Her face like the petals of some pale rose
That is sprinkled with morning dew;
Round her heavenly form her light dress blows
Like a cloud of a misty hue.

"Chłopcze mój piękny, chłopcze mój młody – "My handsome young stripling," so o'er and o'er
Zanuci czule dziewica - Comes the maiden's tender croon,
Po co wokoło Świteziu wody Oh, why do you walk on the desolate shore
Błądzisz przy świetle księżyca? By the light of the shining moon?

"Po co żałujesz dzikiej wietrznicy, "Why do you grieve for a wanton flirt
Która cię zwabia w te knieje, Who has cozened you into her trap,
Zawraca głowę, rzuca w tęsknicy Who has turned your head and has brought you to hurt
I może jeszcze się śmieje ? And who laughs at you now, mayhap?

Daj się namówić czułym wyrazem, "Oh, heed my soft words and my gentle glance,
Porzuć wzdychania i żale, Sigh and be mournful no more,
Do mnie tu, do mnie, tu będziem razem But come to me here and together we'll dance
Po wodnym pląsać krysztale. On the water's crystal floor.

Czy zechcesz niby jaskółka chybka "You may fly like the swallow that swiftly skims,
Oblicze tylko wód muskać; Just brushing the water's face,
Czy zdrów jak rybka, wesół jak rybka, Oh, merry and sound as a fish, you may swim
Cały dzień ze mną się pluskać. All day in the splashing race.

A na noc w łożu srebrnej topieli "You may sleep in the silvery depths at night
Pod namiotami zwierciadeł, On a couch in a mirrored tent
Na miękkiej wodnych lilijek bieli, Upon water lilies soft and white
Śród boskich usnąć widziadeł. Amid visions of ravishment."

Wtem z zasłon błysną piersi łabędzie, Her swan bosom gleams through her drapery
Strzelec w ziemię patrzy skromnie, The hunter's glance nodestly falls
Dziewica w lekkim zbliża się pędzie As the maiden draws nearer him over the sea
I "Do mnie - woła - pójdź do mnie". And "Come to me, come!" she calls.

I na wiatr lotne rzuciwszy stopy, Then winging her path on the breeze she sweeps
Jak tęcza śmiga w krąg wielki, In a rainbow arch away
To znowu siekąc wodne zatopy, And cutting the waves in the watery deeps
Srebrnymi pryska kropelki. She splashes the silver spray.

Podbiega strzelec i staje w biegu, The youth follows after, then pauses once more,
I chciałby skoczyć, i nie chce; He would leap yet he still draws back;
Wtem modra fala prysnąwszy z brzegu And the damp wave goes rippling away from the shore,
z lekka mu w stopy załechce. Luring him on in its track.

I tak go łechce, i tak go znęca, It lures him caressingly over the sand
Tak się w nim serce rozpływa, Till his heart melts away in his breast,
Jak gdy tajemnie rękę młodzieńca As when a chaste maid softly presses the hand
Ściśnie kochanka wstydliwa. Of the youth whom she loves the best.

Zapomniał strzelec o swej dziewczynie, No longer he thinks of his own fair maid
Przysięgą pogardził świętą, And the vow that he swore he would keep;
Na zgubę oślep bieży w głębinie, By another enchantress his senses are swayed
Nową zwabiony ponętą. And he runs to his death in the deep.

Bieży i patrzy, patrzy i bieży; He hastens and gazes, he looks and he hastes,
Niesie go wodne przestworze, Till already the land is far;
Już z dala suchych odbiegł wybrzeży, He is carried away on the lake's broad wastes
Na średnim igra jeziorze. Where its midmost waters are.

I już dłoń śnieżną w swej ciśnie dłoni, Now his fingers clasp snowy-cool fingertips,
W pięknych licach topi oczy, His eyes meet a beautiful face,
Ustami usta różane goni, He presses his lips against rosy lips,
I skoczne okręgi toczy. And he circles through dancing space.

Wtem wietrzyk świsnął, o bloczek pryska,	Then a little breeze whistled, a little cloud broke
Co ją w łudzącym krył blasku,	That had cast its deceiving shade,
Poznaje strzelec dziewczynę z bliska:	And the youth knows the maid, now unhid by its cloak
Ach, to dziewczyna spod lasku!	'Tis his love of the woodland glade!

A gdzie przysięga ? gdzie moja rada ?
Wszak kto przysięgę naruszy,
Ach, biada jemu, za życia biada!
I biada jego złej duszy!

"Now where is my counsel and where is your oath
And the vow you so solemnly swore?
Oh, woe to the man who has broken it, both
While he lives and forevermore!

Nie tobie igrać przez srebrne tonie
Lub nurkiem pluskać w głąb jasną;
Surowa ziemia ciało pochłonie,
Oczy twe żwirem zagasną.

"Not for you is the silvery whirlpool's cup
Nor the gulfs where the clear sea lies,
But the harsh earth shall swallow your body up
And the gravel shall put out your eyes.

A dusza przy tym świadomym drzewie
Niech lat doczeka tysiąca,
Wiecznie piekielne cierpiąc żarzewie
Nie ma czym zgasić gorąca.

"For a thousand years shall your spirit wait
By the side of this witnessing tree,
And the fires of hell that never abate
Shall burn you unceasingly."

Słyszy to strzelec, błędny krok niesie,
Błędnymi rzuca oczyma.
A wicher szumi po gęstym lesie,
Woda się burzy i wzdyma.

He hears and he walks with a wandering tread,
He gazes with wandering eyes;
Then a hurricane out of the deepwood sped
And the waters seethe and rise.

Burzy się, wzdyma i wre aż do dna,
Kręconym nurtem pochwyca,
Roztwiera paszczę otchłań podwodna,
Ginie z młodzieńcem dziewica.

They seethe to their depths and the circling tide
Of the whirlpool snatches them down
Through its open jaws as the seas divide:
So the youth and the maiden drown.

Woda się dotąd burzy i pieni,
Dotąd przy świetle księżyca
Snuje się para znikomych cieni:
jest to z młodzieńcem dziewica.

And still when the lake waters foam and roar,
And still in the moon's pale light,
Two shadows come flitting along the shore:
The youth and the maiden bright.

Ona po srebrnym pląsa jeziorze,
On pod tym jęczy modrzewiem.
Któż jest młodzieniec? - strzelcem był w borze.
A kto dziewczyna? - ja nie wiem.

She plays where the lake glitters silver and clear,
He groans by the old larch tree;
The youth hunted game in the forest here,
But the maiden is strange to me.[1]

12 sierpnia 1821

[1]English translation by George Rapall Noyes in *Poems by Adam Mickiewicz*, 1944.

Breinigsville, PA USA
03 September 2009
223525BV00001B/102/P